MEGHAN

DUCHESS OF SUSSEX

QUEEN OF STYLE

Danann
BOOKS

Danann BOOKS

First Published Danann Publishing Ltd 2019

WARNING: For private domestic use only, any unauthorised Copying, hiring, lending or public performance of this book is illegal.

CAT NO: DAN0433

Photography courtesy of

Getty images:

- Jack Taylor / Stringer
- Amanda Edwards / Stringer
- Neilson Barnard
- Angela Weiss / Stringer
- Mark Cuthbert
- Mike Mcgregor / Stringer
- Brad Barket
- Darren Mccollester / Stringer
- Alberto E. Rodriguez
- Janette Pellegrini / Stringer
- Max Mumby/Indigo
- Chris Jackson
- Daniel Leal-Olivas
- Steve Back
- Kirsty Wigglesworth - Pool
- Mark Metcalfe / Stringer
- Andrew Milligan - WPA Pool

- Victoria Jones
- Eddie Mulholland - WPA Pool
- Charlotte Graham - WPA Pool
- Andrew Parsons - Pool
- MPI99/Bauer-Griffin
- Lars Niki
- Steve Parsons - Pool
- Ben Birchall - WPA Pool
- Andrew Matthews - WPA Pool
- Ben Stansall
- Yui Mok
- Ben Stansall - WPA Pool
- Hannah Mckay - Pool
- Dominic Lipinski
- Eddie Mulholland - WPA Pool
- Ian Vogler
- Hagen Hopkins

- Paul Edwards - Pool
- Adrian Dennis
- Nick Bradshaw
- Phil Noble - Pool
- Ian Vogler - Pool
- Ryan Pierse
- Francois Durand / Stringer
- Clive Mason
- Andy Buchanan
- Pool/Max Mumby
- Saeed Khan
- Joe Maher/BFC
- Niklas Halle'n
- Jon Bond - WPA Pool
- Neil Mockford
- James D. Morgan
- Darrian Traynor

Book layout & design Darren Grice at Ctrl-d

Made in EU.

ISBN: 978-1-912332-39-7

CONTENTS

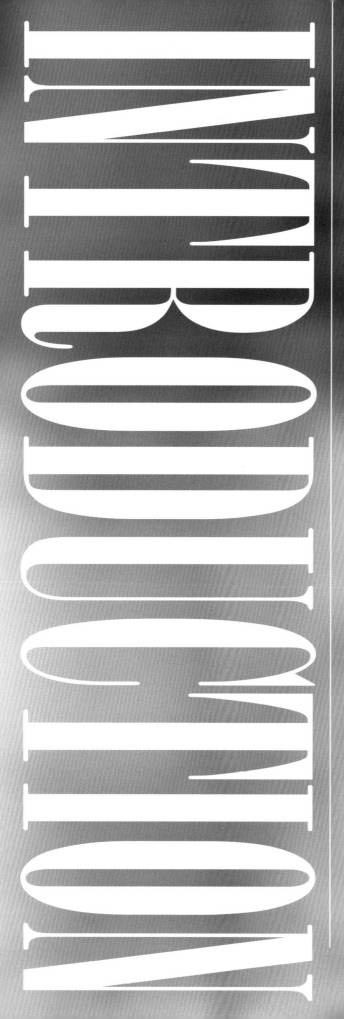

INTRODUCTION

'I love the
opportunity to get
properly dressed up'

Meghan Markle

From striped blazers to crisp button-down shirts, off-the-shoulder jackets to tailored tuxedos, trench-style dresses to bespoke handbags and headpieces, slinky leather skirts to sophisticated ball gowns, magnificently tailored coats to to-die for shoes... Meghan, Duchess of Sussex is rapidly become fashion's ruling queen of style. A bona fide fashionista before she joined the House of Windsor, Meghan has become a global style icon, renowned for her contemporary, elegant and occasionally edgy aesthetic. She is breaking the mould when it comes to Royal fashion. She is also breaking the internet. The websites of her favoured designers crash within minutes of her wearing an item while the off-the-peg garments she favours sell out just as rapidly. *'Meghan – Duchess of Sussex, Queen of Style'* charts her fashion sense and style evolution from her classic *'California girl'* youth and years as struggling actress through to her days as a *'Deal or No Deal'* TV hostess, becoming the star of successful legal drama *'Suits'* and now as a Royal Duchess – arguably the most fashion-literate, style-savvy Royal there has ever been...

The Duchess of Sussex visits the Hubb Community Kitchen to see how funds raised by the 'Together: Our Community' Cookbook are making a difference at Al Manaar, North Kensington on November 21, 2018

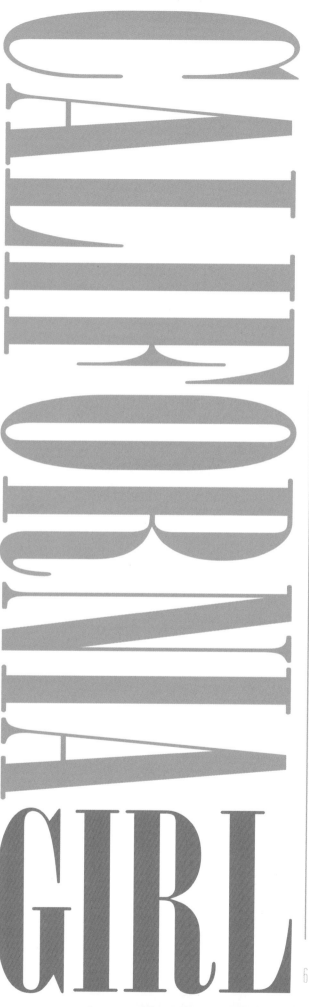

CALIFORNIA GIRL

'Make way for the Royal Highness'

The nine-year-old Meghan Markle pretending to be a queen in a childhood game

August 4 1981 and in London, England, Queen Elizabeth the Queen Mother was celebrating her 81st birthday. At the same time, 5,500 miles away in Canoga Park, Los Angeles, California, USA, a biracial baby girl was being born who, 36 years later, would marry Prince Harry, the Queen Mother's great grandson. At the time, such a union would have been regarded as fantasy.

The baby's mother was one Doria Ragland, a 24-year-old African American who two years earlier had married divorced TV lighting designer Thomas Markle, some 12 years her senior. They had met in 1978 when she was a temp at ABC television and he was working as a lighting director on a US soap opera.

'I like to think he was drawn to her sweet eyes and her Afro,' commented their daughter in 2016.

Doria and Thomas, who already had two teenage kids from his first marriage, were besotted with their baby whom they nicknamed *'Bud'* or *'Flower'*. Her official name was Rachel Meghan Markle, although she was known as Meghan. The family settled in

Woodland Hills, a prosperous Los Angeles neighbourhood and all seemed well at first. However, Doria and Thomas's marriage was in trouble – not helped by the fact that in the largely white neighbourhood in which they lived, Doria was constantly mistaken for the hired help.

'There was my mom, caramel in complexion with her light-skinned baby in tow, being asked where my mother was since they assumed she was the nanny,' Meghan has said.

When their little *'Flower'* was just two years old, Doria and Thomas split. Being so young, the break-up of their marriage seemed not to affect her – especially as her parents were always careful to put on a united front.

'What's so incredible, you know, is that my parents split up when I was two, but I never saw them fight. We would still take vacations together and my dad would come on Sundays to drop me off. We were still so close-knit,' she said.

On weekdays, Doria had her daughter living with her while Thomas had custo dy at weekends. It was at this time that Meghan was enrolled in the kindergarten of the prestigious Little Red School House, where many Hollywood stars chose to send their children. She would stay at the school until she was 11. A bright child, Meghan was already very aware of her mixed-race heritage – as were her parents. When she was seven, her father imaginatively created a very special gift for her.

'On Christmas morning, swathed in glitter-flecked wrapping paper, there I found my Heart Family: a black mom doll, a white dad doll, and a child in each colour,' she has written. *'My dad had taken the sets apart and customized my family.'*

For seventh grade, Meghan, although a non-Catholic, moved to the private, all-girls Immaculate Heart High School where she immediately showed an intelligence and sensibility beyond her years.

'There was a mandatory census I had to complete in my English class – you had to check one of the boxes to indicate your ethnicity: white, black, Hispanic or Asian,' she has recalled. *'There I was (my curly hair, my freckled face, my pale skin, my mixed race) looking down at these boxes, not wanting to mess up, but not knowing what to do. You could only choose one, but that would be to choose one parent over the other – and one half of myself over the other. My teacher told me to check the box for Caucasian. "Because that's how you look, Meghan," she said. I put down my pen. Not as an act of defiance, but rather a symptom of my confusion. I couldn't bring myself to do that, to picture the pit-in-her-belly sadness my mother would feel if she were to find out. So, I didn't tick a box. I left my identity blank – a question mark, an absolute incomplete – much like how I felt. When I went home that night, I told my dad what had happened. He said the words that have always stayed with me: "If that happens again, you draw your own box."'*

Aged just 12, Meghan also showed her mettle against corporate giant Procter & Gamble. Watching commercials on TV, she was deeply unhappy because an advertisement for a P&G dish washing liquid was sexist, citing that the women of America were in uproar over their dirty pots and pans. She wrote letters to Proctor & Gamble, then First Lady Hillary Clinton and Linda Ellerbee, the then executive producer and anchor of *"Nick News,"* on the Nickelodeon Children's TV Channel. Clinton replied with praise, the company changed the wording of the ad and Ellerbee profiled the young Meghan on TV.

'I don't think it's right for kids to grow up thinking that mom does

everything,' said pre-teen Meghan in the interview. *'It's always mom does this and mom does that. My parents always told me if I believed something was wrong, I should try to fix it.'*

Ellerbee, for one, was deeply impressed.

'I knew after that story that this little girl wasn't going to change,' she says. *'Rather that she was going to change her world.'*

Christine Knudsen, a teacher at the Immaculate Heart, saw that same steely determination in the young Meghan.

'She didn't see things as roadblocks – and I think she loved to rise to challenges,' Knudsen commented. *'And, "OK, this door is closed. Let's find a window."'*

Meghan deliberately busied herself with activities at school because she felt she didn't really fit in.

'My high school had the cliques – the black girls, the white girls, the Latino girls,' she later said. *'Being biracial, I fell somewhere in between. So, every day, during lunch, I busied myself with meetings: French club, student body, whatever one could possibly do between noon and 1pm – I was there. Not so I was more involved but so I wouldn't have to eat alone. In middle school and high school, there was this huge span of my life where I was just the girl with the crazy curly hair, a big gap between my teeth and skinny legs. I was always the smart one. My self-identification was wrapped up in being the smart one.'*

She was also charitable and had been raised to think of others.

'My parents came from little, so they made a choice to give a lot: buying turkeys for homeless shelters at Thanksgiving, delivering meals to people in hospices, giving spare change to those asking for it,' she revealed in 2015. *'I started working at a soup kitchen in skid row of Los Angeles when I was 13 years old, and the first day, I felt really scared. I was young, and it was rough and raw down there, and though I was with a great volunteer group, I just felt overwhelmed.'*

From the age of 13, Meghan was encouraged to work as a server and table clearer at the Hippie Kitchen charity in downtown Los Angeles.

It was while she was in her teens – 15 to be exact - that Meghan took her first trip outside the US – to Europe with her closest friend Ninaki Priddy and family. A now famous photograph shows Meghan – in a simple black dress and converse slider shoes, looking very much like typical '90s teenager – posing outside Buckingham Palace. She could have never known then that she would enter its gates 21 years later as the fiancée of a prince.

From a tender age, Meghan had dreamed of becoming an actress and being a pupil at the Immaculate Heart only fuelled this ambition. She starred in several school productions including *'Damn Yankees!', 'Annie', 'Stage Door'* and *'Into The Woods'* before graduating in 1999. She was considered a star in the making.

'Meghan was really charismatic and was a very hard worker and very focused and you could tell she was going to do something special with her life… ,' a former schoolmate of hers has commented. *'She had the talent and focus to back it up and you could tell she knew the work it would take and she was willing to put in the work.'*

Former child actress Gigi Perreau, who helped direct productions at the Immaculate Heart and taught drama classes there, was of the same opinion.

'We never had a moment's problem with her – she was spot on, learned her lines when she had to, very dedicated, very focused. She was a wonderful student, a lovely girl even then and very hard working. I wasn't sure which direction Meghan would ultimately be going in because she also had interests in humanitarian activities. She had a good heart, had absorbed the school's philosophy that there is nothing we cannot do, and she seemed to be focused on her future. She was very dedicated. I knew she would be something special.'

Meghan's years at Immaculate Heart High ended on a high. Describing herself as *'classy'* in her final Year Book entry, she was crowned Home Coming Queen at her last school prom which was held with all-boys school, St Francis. Dressed in a baby-blue gown, carrying a bouquet and wearing a tiara, Meghan looked like a princess already.

In August 1999, Meghan left her native California to attend Northwestern University in Illinois, where she had decided to study English rather than drama, feeling that the latter was something of a clichéd option for a girl from LA. Having had the gap in her front teeth fixed, Meghan had decided how she would style herself at Northwestern. She wanted a smart, sophisticated look and opted for mainly black, white and grey pencil skirts, tube tops and structured blouse/jackets – a forerunner of the *'Rachel Zane'* style she would adopt in *'Suits'* some years later.

At Northwestern University, Meghan joined the Kappa Kappa Gamma sorority – whose members were described as, *'Intelligent, hot messes… very driven, ambitious and passionate'* and participated in community service and charity projects. As at high school, her contemporaries had noticed her charismatic personality and how sophisticated and put together she was.

'I just always remember saying that she, like, looked like a princess, I don't know how else to describe it,' says sorority sister Erica Bethe Levin. *'She just radiated like, this, ridiculous aura.'*

Meghan's love of politics and current affairs saw her changing her major from English to a dual major of Theatre Arts and International Relations – indicating some indecision about how she saw her future. Would she become an actress, political activist or perhaps a diplomat? Taking some time out from Northwestern, she served an internship at the American embassy in Buenos Aires, Argentina, and studied for a semester in Madrid, Spain. In 2003, Meghan received a bachelor's degree from Northwestern's School of Communication in 2003, with her double major achieved. She then returned home to Los Angeles, her mind made up about a career. She wanted to become a successful Hollywood actress – a star – and nothing would stand in her way.

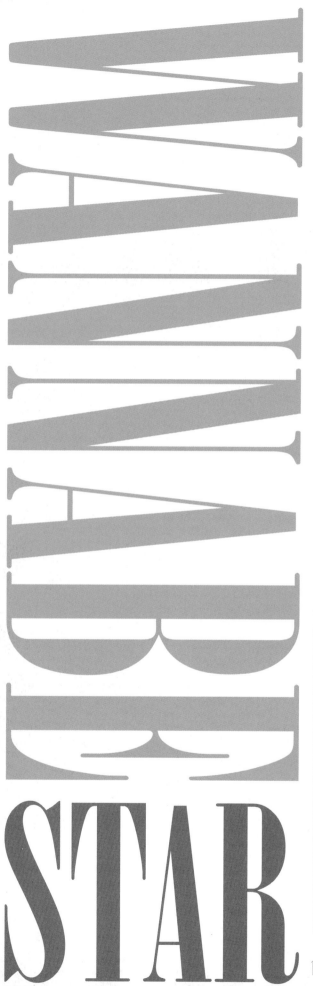

WANNABE STAR

'My closet was filled with fashionable frocks to make me look as racially varied as an Eighties Benetton poster.'

Meghan on her noughties style

Life as a young actress in Hollywood was tough. Thanks to her father's contacts in the industry Meghan, while still a student, had been employed as a *'day player'* in the soap *'General Hospital'*. Playing Nurse Jill and wearing blue scrubs, she was rewarded with five lines of dialogue. She'd also appeared in a couple of music videos. But now she was back in LA for good and doing it *'for real'*, it was audition after audition after audition for commercials, movies and TV shows. It was good experience but hardly fulfilling as the roles continued to elude her. As at school and then college, the audition process also highlighted Meghan's *'ethnic ambiguity'* which she was later to talk about.

'There couldn't possibly be a more label-driven industry than acting, seeing as every audition comes with a character breakdown: "Beautiful, sassy, Latina, 20s"; "African American, urban, pretty, early 30s"; "Caucasian, blonde, modern girl next door". Every role has a label; every casting is for something specific. Being "ethnically ambiguous" I was pegged in the industry, meaning I could audition for virtually any role. Morphing from Latina when I was dressed in red, to African American when in mustard yellow; my closet filled with fashionable frocks to make me look as racially varied as an

Meghan Markle attends the DPA pre-Emmy Gift Lounge at the Peninsula Hotel on September 18, 2009 in Beverly Hills, California

Meghan Markle attends the DPA pre-Emmy Gift Lounge at the Peninsula Hotel on September 18, 2009 in Beverly Hills, California

Eighties Benetton poster. Sadly, it didn't matter: I wasn't black enough for the black roles and I wasn't white enough for the white ones, leaving me somewhere in the middle as the ethnic chameleon who couldn't book a job.'

Many out-of-work or wannabe actresses waited tables, but Meghan's innate classiness and a talent for calligraphy meant that she could earn a living another way while she waited for acting roles to come up and the auditions to come good.

'I went to an all-girls' Catholic school for, like, six years during the time when kids actually had handwriting class and have always had a propensity for getting the cursive down pretty well,' she told an interviewer in 2013. *'What it evolved into was my pseudo-waitressing job when I was auditioning. I did calligraphy for the invitations for, like, Robin Thicke and Paula Patton's wedding. I used to do it for Dolce & Gabbana's celebrity correspondence. I would sit there with a little white tube sock on my hand so no hand oils got on the card, trying to pay my bills while auditioning.'*

She also earned a little extra by acting as a hostess in a Beverley Hills restaurant and working at a local store where she taught how to gift wrap. This might have deflated a less resilient character but Meghan refused to become despondent. A child of Hollywood, she was aware of the pitfalls of the profession she so wished to be a part of and so decided to *'stay happy'*. It was around this time – 2004 – that she met the man who would become her first husband. A gregarious New York born and raised producer and director, Trevor Engleson, like Meghan, was determined to *'make it'* in Hollywood. At five years her senior, the savvy Engleson enthralled Meghan and it was one of his many sayings that she adopted for herself – *'Don't give it five minutes unless you can give it five years'* – in relation to forging a successful career in Hollywood. The 6' 5" strawberry blond was handsome, intelligent, funny and caring – and definitely

had the connections to help make Meghan's aspirations come true. They were a would-be *'Power Couple'* resolved to take the movie and TV worlds by storm.

In 2004 Meghan landed her first movie role in a film called *'A Lot Like Love'*, starring heartthrob Ashton Kutcher. Initially she was given just one line but so impressed the director, he allowed her to improvise four more. She was credited only as *'Hot Girl'*. Her next role was in a science-fiction legal drama which aired only five episodes, but it allowed Meghan to say that she had acted alongside future Oscar and Emmy winner Viola Davis. She was then cast in a tiny, one-line role in the sitcom *'Cuts'*. At this point, Meghan finally felt her career was taking off and described this feeling in the anonymous blog *'Working Actress'* which she is thought to have written.

'At the start of my career, I remember freaking out, and celebrating over getting one line on a sh***y show. At the time that was a big success. It was phone calls of congrats, and flowers and celebratory dinners with wine glasses clinking. It was a landmark of more work to come, and a glimmer of hope that said "Holy s**t, you're really doing this".'

Her next job was hardly what she'd had in mind, however. In 2006 Meghan became a provocatively dressed *'Briefcase Girl'* on TV game show *'Deal or No Deal'*.

'Working on "Deal or No Deal" was a learning experience, and it helped me to understand what I would rather be doing,' she later recalled. *'I would end up standing up there forever in these terribly uncomfortable and inexpensive five-inch heels just waiting for someone to pick my number so I could go and sit down. I didn't ever have it. I don't think I did. I was the ill-fated number 26, which for some reason no one would ever choose. I would put it in the category of things I was doing while I was auditioning to try to make ends meet.'*

Model and TV presenter Chrissy Teigan was one of Meghan's fellow 'Briefcase Girls'.

'Yes, I was on "Deal or No Deal" with her and she was lovely,' says Teigan. *'Now everyone asks me what she was like and I say, "Sorry, no dirt". She's gorgeous.'*

For Meghan, the gig was but a temporary one. She was determined to make it as an actress. In 2007, she was cast as stripper and streetwalker Kelly in the pilot of new TV drama, *'The Apostles'*. Meghan had a good feeling about the role and the show but, after much deliberating by the networks, unfortunately it was not picked up. She felt desolate and described the feeling in her Working Actress blog.

'I'm not gonna lie. I've spent many days curled up in bed with a loaf of bread and some wine. A one-woman pity party. It's awful and ridiculous.'

Meghan picked herself up, brushed herself down and started all over again. She went on to land minor roles in *'Without a Trace'*, *'90210'*, *'CSI'* and *'Fringe'*, in which, as Junior FBI Agent Amy Jessup, Meghan was able to experience some of the excitement that comes with acting in television crime dramas.

'We did a month of gun training, kicking down doors, and it's such a departure from who I am. That's the fun part of our job — to be able to play dress up, and to really throw yourself into something you otherwise wouldn't,' she related in a magazine interview.

The year 2009, saw Meghan landing a small, uncredited part in the movie *'Get Him to the Greek'*. However, she had a starring role as Trevor's real-life, long-term partner. Stylish, beautiful and supportive, Meghan wowed the crowds as she walked the red carpet with him at a famous Hollywood club which threw a party in his honour after he was the subject of a glowing write-up in *'Hollywood Reporter'*. Trevor's career was flying and he found roles for his girlfriend in two projects, *'The Candidate'* – a short film about an underhand company man offered assistance by a secret organisation that immerses him in forces beyond his control – and the 9/11 based *'Remember Me'*. Meghan had a small part in this Robert Pattinson movie, where she played a bartender named Megan. Speaking about starring in the film and co-starring with R-Patz she said, *'I filmed some scenes in New York with him for a small part. He's a really lovely guy and a really great example to be able to watch someone who is young, who's stardom has really taken over his life in such a huge way, and yet he's still gracious, humble and cool. I think that is really endearing.'*

Meghan longed for stardom to take over her life. In 2010, she landed a 35-second scene in the comedy movie *'Horrible Bosses'* where she was cast as a Fed Ex employee and, on screen, described as *'too cute for Fed Ex'* by the movie's star, Jason Sudeikis. It wasn't enough. She needed a break. Now in her late 20s, in her heart of hearts Meghan knew that time was running out. She'd given it far longer than five years but was still a long way off *'making it'*. She may have been LA born-and-bred with the entertainment industry hardwired in her DNA, but how much longer could she cope with the relentless round of hope and disappointment? Then in summer 2010, she auditioned for the role of paralegal Rachel Zane in a new show the USA Network were developing – a legal drama called *'Suits'*.

Meghan Markle arrives at the Anti-Defamation League Entertainment Industry Awards Dinner at the Beverly Hilton on October 11, 2011 in Beverly Hills, California

THE SUITS YEARS

Meghan Markle in 2016

It was on the way to attending the audition for *'Suits'* that Meghan had a sudden brainwave. She was dressed in a plum-coloured spaghetti strap top, black jeans and high heels, but was this really the kind of outfit an ambitious, stylish character like Rachel Zane would wear to work? Meghan decided not. To appear more lawyer-like, Meghan dashed into an H&M store and bought a simple black dress to change into once she arrived at the studio. It was a genius move. As soon as he saw her in her smart black dress, *'Suits'* creator Aaron Korsh knew he'd found his Rachel, while USA Network Executive Jeff Watchell commented on Meghan's urbane edge and the chemistry she had with her co-star, Patrick J Adams, who was to play Rachel's love interest, Mike Ross.

Meghan was delighted yet cautious to learn the role of Rachel's was hers and that the pilot would start shooting that autumn. In seven years, she had made five pilots but none had been picked up. But it turned out to be sixth time lucky for Meghan and the rest of the *'Suits'* team. In January 2011, the project got the green light. Shooting the first series would start that April. It was a busy year as in September Meghan and Trevor were married, having become engaged in late 2010. A four-day celebration took place in

SHOPSTYLE

Meghan Markle attends an exclusive preview of the Marchesa Voyage for ShopStyle collection on September 5, 2014 in New York City

Ocho Rios, Jamaica, with the bride wearing a strapless white gown with bejewelled belt feature. Although set in New York, *'Suits'* was filmed in Toronto, which meant the newly wed Meghan relocating permanently to the Canadian metropolis once the show had been commissioned for a second series. Trevor remained in Los Angeles. It wasn't the ideal start to married life, but both Meghan and Trevor seemed confident that their union would survive the separation.

Fashion was at the heart of the *'Suits'* narrative – much as it had been with that other style-centric drama *'Sex and the City'* – and Rachel Zane, and therefore Meghan, became the show's muse. Her on-screen look had to tick all the boxes. Costume designer Jolie Andreatta rejoiced in dressing Rachel, while Meghan rejoiced in wearing designer clothes.

'Meghan and I loved Rachel's clothes,' revealed Andreatta. *'We'd always say that, if we could, we would live in Rachel's clothes. Designing Rachel's look was like being a kid in a candy store.'*

A crisp collared shirt was a mainstay in Rachel Zane's wardrobe, often paired with a sleek pencil skirt or tailored trousers. There were high heel court shoes, form-fitting dresses with flattering cuts and trench coat-style dresses – all in chic tonal colour palettes of caramel, soft pink, cream and brown or monochrome. It was the ultimate in *'classy'* and Meghan's own look altered as a result.

'I think it's really changed because my sensibility had always been relaxed California girl style, and on any given day I was in jeans, cut-offs and flip-flops,' she said. *'But the weather alone in Toronto changes your wardrobe! The fashion on "Suits" is gorgeous, so it also became my education of designers and really knowing what fits my body well. On "Suits" I'm dressed in Alexander McQueen, Tom Ford, and Prada almost every day. Now what I'm starting to learn is, even though things look amazing on the hanger, it doesn't mean they're going to look amazing on me. For example, I love Victoria Beckham dresses, but I don't have the long torso to support that silhouette.'*

Meghan's star was on the rise – and so was her style. An anonymous Hollywood source claims that Meghan celebrated her rise to fame with a *'Sayonara Zara'* party. During the event, she supposedly gave away her old, inexpensive clothes to guests, making room for the newer and pricier options she could now afford. She was certainly

Actress Meghan Markle attends ELLE's Annual Women in Television Celebration at Sunset Tower on January 22, 2014 in West Hollywood, California

becoming something of a style icon – and guru – and was asked constantly about her fashion sense.

'I think one of the key tips for looking polished is tailoring,' she advised in one interview. *'No matter what you get, if it's budget or high-end, if you have it tailored for your body you're going to look 10 times better. Stick to what makes you feel best. Have a power piece in your wardrobe. If it's the one dress that makes you feel so badass, or the one crisp button-down – whatever it is so that when you wake up on those days where you're not really feeling like going into work, you put that piece on and it's almost like your own anthem. It can really shift the energy of your whole day. I think our clothes are such a reflection of how we're feeling. A lot of my personal style is reflected in Rachel's look – I like monochromatic and tonal dressing and I don't generally wear prints, and neither does Rachel now. Rachel wears a lot of separates – she's really the only character on the show who you'll see mix and match wardrobe basics like a normal person would.'*

When invited to appear on the red carpet or at a fashion show, Meghan favoured mini-dresses that showed off her legs, body-conscious silhouettes, and even the occasional gala-worthy gown – like the velvet Stella McCartney cocktail dress she wore when MC-ing the Anti-Defamation League Entertainment Industry Awards dinner at the Beverly Hilton Hotel in Hollywood with husband Trevor at her side.

But as time went on, it transpired that Trevor – or rather the marriage – was a casualty of Meghan's growing fame. Less than two years after their Jamaican wedding, Meghan filed for divorce, citing irreconcilable differences. It's not known what these differences were, exactly. Some sources maintained that the pressures of their long-distance relationship became too much while others hinted at Meghan's desire to be a single now that she was successful. Whatever… the marriage was over. Meghan concentrated on *'Suits'*, enjoying Toronto and making firm friends with the city's high-profile residents, such as fashion stylist Jessica Mulroney, and, in 2014, starting her lifestyle blog, *'The TIG'*. Named after her favourite red wine, Italian Tignanello, the blog was a place where Meghan shared various aspects of her life and the things that inspired her. In her own words, *'The TIG is a hub for the discerning palate - those*

Meghan Markle attends the London Global Gift Gala at ME Hotel on November 19, 2013 in London, England

In 2015, Meghan's fashion profile was furthered heightened when she became a brand ambassador for Canadian department store, Reitmans, in an attempt to re-energize the brand. She was thrilled.

'Being born and raised in L.A., I wasn't familiar with the brand, but what I loved is what they're trying to do – they're a family-owned business for 90 years and it's time for a bit of re-energizing,' she said. *'They'll still have all the classics but a little bit hipper, a little bit more chic – pieces that are a bit more trend-driven. I love the idea of being a part of something like that. I felt really honoured that they asked me to be the face of this campaign.'*

Not long after becoming an ambassador, the store approached Meghan again and asked her to design a capsule collection of dresses. In a post on The TIG she described her inspiration and what she wanted her collection to include.

'I conceived the dress capsule as four distinct pieces that you could have in your closet, or throw in your suitcase and be confident and covered for any event. I toiled over design and print, I shared my thoughts on everything (come on guys, you know I'm opinionated), and I ended up with a limited collection of pieces that reflect facets of my personal style that I think (hope, pray, hold-my-breath-and-wait-for-the-comments-on-Insta), that you'll love.'

All outfits in the collection retailed for less than £100. The first dress *'clearly inspired by Rachel Zane'* as was *'The Soiree'*. Described as *'elegant and feminine'* with a *'silhouette-conscious bodice… styled with cold-shoulder cut-outs'* this *'little black number'* was designed to *'ensure every night's a bit of an adventure'*.

Meghan revealed *'The Sunset'* dress reminded her of *'everything about growing up in LA'*. The printed maxi dress featured a *'dramatic flowing shape complimented by a stylish open back detail'* and promised to add *'undeniable style to your days and nights.'*

'The Date Night' made Meghan feel *'fashion-y and Frenchie'*, featuring an *'elegant halter top, bare shoulders, and bold, rich colour (red dahlia)'*

Meghan Markle attends the Annual Charity Day Hosted By Cantor Fitzgerald and BGC at the Cantor Fitzgerald Office on September 11, 2013 in New York, United States

for a unique style. The dress was described as *'irresistibly soft and flirty so you can go with the flow no matter what the plans are.'*

Meghan's *'Terrace Dress'* was billed as the *'dress that will replace your LBD – because you need the perfect: Little. White. Dress'*. The sleeveless dress was styled with a *'v-neckline, a fitted top, and an asymmetric skirt'* and perfect for *'a cocktail here, there, and everywhere'*.

Meghan was delighted with the result.

'I'm really excited,' she blogged. *'It's the first time I've ever designed. I've been involved in every facet of the design process, so it's really personal. It's a huge moment, especially because I feel like I've adopted Canada as much as it's adopted me in the past five years.'*

Meghan's dress collection became available in April 2016 and was an instant sell-out! Her second collection was released that November. Consisting of five workwear pieces in muted colours of white, grey, and black, the mix-and-match collection reflected, *'Markle's aesthetic, as well as her ambition to create and collect clothing pieces that will become staples in a wardrobe, and therefore stand the test of time.'* However, the emphasis was on affordability.

'It's a reflection of where I've come from,' said Meghan. *'I've always shopped on the sale rack and I've always been the girl flipping through the hangers trying to find the best deal. And now, being able to say, wow, this has my name on it and is at a price point that I think is really approachable and I'm proud to say a lot of people can afford. And also that it's an accurate reflection of my personal style, and also the style of my character on "Suits" is awesome. I'm really, really proud of the design process. I've been really grateful to work with Reitmans and have them be patient with me on knowing the craftsmanship I am after and the price point we are both after. And we have been able to come up with an amazing marriage of those two things."*

The first item in this collection was *'The Shirt'* and was described as having *'an oversized fit that's cut just right'* which promised to be a *'new go-to, easy-yet-polished wardrobe favourite'*. It featured a button front, high-low hem, *'trendy dolman sleeves'* and came in lacy white and dark grey. *'The Bodysuit'*, a long-sleeved turtleneck – featuring a snap gusset

Meghan Markle attends AOL Build Presents 'Suits' at AOL Studios In New York on March 17, 2016 in New York City

closure – which came in black, was described as *'undeniably trendy with an autumnal twist'* and would take *'any outfit to the next level'*.

To accompany the tops, the collection featured two leather pieces. The *'Faux Leather Leggings'* had an elastic waistband for an easy pull-on style and were *'sleek and stylish with a hint of stretch'*. *'People don't need to feel scared about a leather pant,'* wrote Meghan. *'Think of it as a jean alternative, it's the same thing. It's almost like they're your yoga pants, but they look chic. I've crafted them to be just that comfortable. You can literally jump on a plane in them, go for a walk with your friends in them, throw them on and go for brunch – they don't need to feel fancy. Put on a sweater and really great sneakers with a big scarf and you'll look so stylish. For me, they are an everyday essential.'*

The *'Faux Leather Skirt'* was also made of the *'smooth-to-the-touch faux leather that looks (and feels) as good as the real thing'*. The pencil skirt, with back vent and zip closure, was marketed as being perfect for *'endless work-to-weekend wearing'*. The final piece of the collection was the *'Cashmere Blend Poncho'* in tonal *'Light Latte'* and *'Charcoal Heather'* shades. The versatile piece could be styled *'belted, as a scarf or in a symmetric way'* and promised to help the wearer *'stay stylish as the weather cools'*. Again, the collection was a sell-out.

Fashion, style and fun, *'Suits'* and *'The TIG'* apart, Meghan was involving herself in charity work. She became a counsellor for the international charity *'One Young World'* and, at the 2014 summit in Dublin, spoke on the topics of gender equality and modern-day slavery. In the same year, she also toured Afghanistan and Spain with the United Services Organisations. In 2016, she travelled to Rwanda as a global ambassador for the Clean Water Campaign, and visited India in order to raise awareness on women's issues. Meghan also worked with the United Entity for Gender Equality and the Empowerment of Women as an Advocate.

Soon after divorcing Trevor, Meghan had begun a relationship with Canadian celebrity chef Cory Vitiello, but by summer 2016, it was over. At something of a loose end, she decided to visit London in order to publicise *'Suits'* and also watch her friend Serena Williams play tennis at Wimbledon. It was during this trip that Meghan went on a blind date that would ultimately change the course of her life forever.

Meghan Markle attends REEBOK #HonorYourDays at Reebok Headquarters on April 28, 2016 in Canton, Massachusetts

OPP. PAGE:

Meghan Markle arrives at the GQ Men of the Year Party at Chateau Marmont on November 13, 2012 in Los Angeles, California

ABOVE L:

Meghan Markle attends the London Global Gift Gala at ME Hotel on November 19, 2013 in London, England

ABOVE R:

Meghan Markle attends the Annual Charity Day Hosted By Cantor Fitzgerald and BGC at the Cantor Fitzgerald Office on September 11, 2013 in New York

ROYAL COURTSHIP & ENGAGEMENT

'Nothing about me has changed. I'm still the same person.'

Meghan Markle shortly before her engagement to Prince Harry in November 2017

I t is not known what Meghan wore for her blind date – thought to have been arranged by mutual friend Violet Von Westholz – with HRH Prince Harry of Wales on that July evening in 2016. As it was a casual drink at private members club Soho House, perhaps she sported the *'jeans, nice top and blazer'* she had quoted as being her go-to date night look in an interview given a few years earlier. Whatever her look, Harry was impressed – and clearly smitten. When later asked when he knew Meghan was *'the one'*, he'd replied, *'the first time we met'*, adding, *'I was beautifully surprised when I walked into that room and saw her and there she was sitting there. I thought, I am really going to have to up my game here.'*

Meg han was a little more cautious. *'Because I'm from the States, you don't grow up with the same understanding of the Royal family,'* she later explained. *'I didn't know much about him, so the only thing that I asked was, "Well is he nice?" Cause if he wasn't, it just didn't seem like it would make sense.'*

It turns out that he was extremely nice and they arranged to meet the next day. The couple went on a second date then Prince Harry invited Meghan to accompany him on a trip to Africa just three or four weeks later. *'I managed to persuade her to come and join me*

Meghan, Duchess of Sussex visits the University of Chichester's Engineering and Technology Park on October 3, 2018 in Bognor Regis, England

in Botswana and we camped out with each other under the stars,' he said, describing the whirlwind romance. *'Then we were really by ourselves, which was crucial to me to make sure that we had a chance to get to know each other.'*

Throughout late summer and autumn of 2016, Harry visited Meghan in Toronto whenever possible. She also came to London where the couple were spotted on a number of dates. Shortly after news of their romance had broken, social media users noticed that Meghan was wearing a bright beaded bracelet identical to Harry's in an Instagram snap. According to one source, Harry was *'happier than he'd been for many years'* and that *'there was definitely chemistry between them'.* Meghan's Instagram account became the destination for Royal enthusiasts, who noted the timing of a photo of two bananas spooning. It is thought that by this time, Meghan had met Harry's father, Prince Charles. In September 2016, Meghan was reportedly introduced to the heir to the throne at a Balmoral shooting party to celebrate Harry's 32nd birthday.

Prince Harry and Meghan Markle attend a Wheelchair Tennis match during the Invictus Games 2017 at Nathan Philips Square on September 25, 2017 in Toronto, Canada

'I just couldn't wait to see her.'

In early November 2016, Harry took the unprecedented step of releasing a statement via the Kensington Palace Twitter account, urging the public to respect Meghan's privacy in the wake of some outlets making racist and sexist comments about her. *'This is not a game,'* the statement read. *'It is her life and his.'* Later that month, Harry made a secret detour to visit Meghan in Toronto after a 14-day tour of the Caribbean ended. *'I just couldn't wait to see her,'* he's reported to have said. While at a flower shop in Toronto, Meghan was pictured wearing a 14k gold Maya Brenner Asymmetrical Letter necklace, bearing the letters *'M'* and *'H'*.

In December, the couple were seen picking out a Christmas tree at a London market and then photographed leaving a central London theatre – Meghan stylishly wrapped up against the elements in black jeans, ankle boots and coat, a grey shirt and beany hat. A source close to the Prince revealed that *'Harry is more serious than he ever has been about a woman before'*. It was mutual, with Meghan revealing to a Canadian newspaper that, *'My cup runneth over and I'm the luckiest girl in the world.'*

A major relationship milestone occurred in March 2017 when Harry took Meghan as his plus-one to the wedding of close friend, Tom *'Skippy'* Inskip, in Jamaica. In snatched paparazzi shots, Meghan was pictured looking stunning in an elegant Erdem floral maxi dress and sporting Makita Timothy Glossy Gold sunglasses. The couple were snapped cuddling up and exchanging looks of love. A short while later in consideration of her future, Meghan closed *'The TIG'* with the message: *'To all my TIG friends, after close to three beautiful years on this adventure with you, it's time to say goodbye to The TIG. What began as a passion project (my little engine that could) evolved into an amazing community of inspiration, support, fun and frivolity. You've made my days brighter and filled this experience with so much joy. Keep finding those TIG moments of discovery, keep laughing and taking risks, and keep being "the change you wish to see in the world". Above all, don't ever forget your worth*

Prince Harry and his fiancée US actress Meghan Markle pose for a photograph in the Sunken Garden at Kensington Palace in west London on November 27, 2017, following the announcement of their engagement

- as I've told you time and time again: you, my sweet friend, you are enough. Thank you for everything. Xx.'

In April 2017, Meghan was seen wearing a new ring bearing the letter *'H'* on her left index finger. A month later, Meghan and Harry shared their first public kiss, following Harry's participation in the annual Audi Polo Challenge in Ascot, England. The smooch happened outside the polo fields on a parking lot. Meghan was seen cheering on the prince from the sidelines in a stylish navy-blue dress and white blazer combo. A few days later, the Duchess of Cambridge's sister, Pippa, married James Matthews in Berkshire, and Meghan, wearing a maroon backless gown, attended the evening *'do'* at the Middleton family's Berkshire home – with Harry. In early August, Meghan celebrated her 36th birthday with Harry in London before flying to Botswana together where they went on safari. Shortly after returning from the three-week African trip, Harry took Meghan to Balmoral to meet his grandmother, Queen Elizabeth II, for the first time. In October, the couple went to Buckingham Palace for tea with Her Majesty.

Over a year after they'd started dating, Meghan finally talked about the relationship in a glossy magazine. *'We're two people who are really happy and in love,'* she said. *'We were very quietly dating for about six months before it became news, and I was working during that whole time, and the only thing that changed was people's perception. Nothing about me changed. I'm still the same person that I am, and I've never defined myself by my relationship.'*

On September 24 2017, Meghan and Harry made their first public appearance together at an official Royal event, although, due to Royal protocol, they were seated 18 seats apart. Meghan was spotted cheering on her beau as he joined Canadian Prime Minister Justin Trudeau in opening the annual Invictus Games in her adopted home town, Toronto. For the occasion, Meghan wore a burgundy Aritzia dress with a matching Mackage Baya Moto jacket. The next day Meghan – wearing a pure white Misha Nonoo Husband shirt, First Fray jeans by LA based company Mother Denim, Sarah Flint *'Natalie'* flats and sporting a pair of Finlay and Co *'Percy'* sunglasses – and Harry sat together for a Wheelchair Tennis event at the Invicitus Games.

Just two months after this first public appearance, on November 28 the engagement between Harry and Meghan was officially announced. *'His Royal Highness the Prince of Wales is delighted to announce the engagement of Prince Harry to Ms Meghan Markle. The wedding will take place in Spring 2018. Further details about the wedding day will be announced in due course. His Royal Highness and Ms Markle became engaged in London earlier this month. Prince Harry has informed Her Majesty the Queen and other close members of his family. Prince Harry has also sought and received the blessing of Ms Markle's parents. The couple will live in Nottingham Cottage at Kensington Palace.'*

A short time later, the happy couple stepped out at the Sunken Gardens at Kensington Palace before awaiting cameras and journalists, hand-in-hand and looking very much in love. Channelling a bridal look, Meghan wore a white wrap coat by Canadian brand *'Line the Label'*. John Muscat, co-founder and president of the brand commented, *'She particularly loves this coat. She has it in every other colour – she wears it like a second skin.'* The label's website is said to have crashed when Meghan made her appearance and the coat sold out within minutes. Beneath the coat, Meghan had chosen to wear a bottle-green dress by under-the-radar Italian designer P.A.R.O.S.H.. The company's founder, Paolo Rossello, said it was *'an amazing surprise – a dream'* to see Meghan in the dress, which, again was an immediate sell-out. To complete the look, Meghan wore Aquazzura's *'Matilde'* suede high heels, a style copied by Princess Eugenie when she announced her engagement to Jack Brocklebank in January 2018. She sported *'Les Plaisirs de Birks'* 18k gold earrings featuring white opals in her lobes and a custom-made diamond engagement ring sparkled away on her finger. Harry had designed the piece himself, using one diamond sourced from Botswana and two smaller stones from the late Princess Diana's collection. The ring was then made by court jewellers Cleave & Company. *'The little diamonds are from my mother's jewellery collection, to make sure that she's with us on this crazy journey together.'*

Official engagement photographs followed, taken by Polish photographer Alexi Lubomirski, known for his work in fashion and celebrity and formally known as His Serene Highness Prince Alexi Lubomirski after inheriting the title from his father. In stunning shots that wouldn't have looked out of place in a glossy fashion

Prince Harry and his fiancée US actress Meghan Markle pose for a photograph in the Sunken Garden at Kensington Palace in west London on November 27, 2017, following the announcement of their engagement

magazine, he captured Meghan and her Prince in the grounds
of Frogmore House near Windsor. They posed for a formal shot
on the steps outside the house, with Meghan wearing a Ralph &
Russo couture gown which featured a black and gold beaded and
embroidered see-through top (over a nude lining) and a frothy dark
skirt. *'To be honest, we tried on a couple of different things and that
was just one that she felt comfortable in,'* said Lubomirski. The set
of images also included a black and white shot of Harry wrapping
his fiancée – dressed in a Victoria Beckham cashmere crewneck
sweater – in his winter coat, to keep out the cold while she caressed
his cheek.

**In the months leading up to the wedding, Meghan
would prove herself to be the most stylish, fashion-
savvy Royal since Princess Diana.**

Prince Harry and his fiancée US actress Meghan Markle
pose for a photograph in the Sunken Garden at Kensington
Palace in west London on November 27, 2017, following the
announcement of their engagement

THE DUCHESS DOES

BEAUTY

Meghan's Must-Have
Make-up Items

Mercier
Radiance Foundation Primer

For that flawless, glowing look, Meghan has said she's a fan of Laura Mercier's Radiance Primer.

'It's what I put on every day to give my skin a dewy glow.'

Chanel
Sublimage Le Teint Foundation

This Chanel foundation of one the Duchess' favourites, providing a smooth finish without hiding her natural features.

'I never want to cover my freckles so I just do a "wash" of foundation in certain sections instead of over the entire face.'

Yves Saint Laurent
Touche Éclat

A must-have for Meghan's five-minute face.

'Just Touche Éclat, curled lashes, mascara, Chap Stick, and a little bit of blush.'

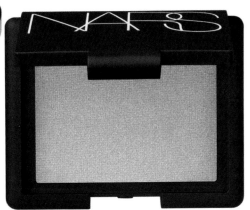

Make Up For Ever
HD Powder

A micro-finishing pressed powder that gives a light matte effect and smooth, luminous finish which Meghan likes to use because:

'it lets your skin look shiny and fresh, but not greasy-shiny.'

NARS
Blush

In 2014 Meghan remarked,

'I love Nars blush — it gives you a nice glow from within.'

MAC
Kohl Eye Pencil in Teddy

A soft pencil liner that lines, defines and shades the eyes with rich colour and a silky smooth, matte/pearl finish.

'If I'm going to vamp it up for the night, then I use MAC Teddy eyeliner, which is a really beautiful brown that has some gold in it.'

Dior Show Iconic
High Definition Lash Curler Mascara

Enriched with a unique lifting formula, Diorshow Iconic sculpts, stretches and curves the lashes with extreme hold and high definition.

'My favourite mascara.'

Revitalash
ADVANCED Eyelash Conditioner

This finely calibrated, scientifically driven cosmetic eyelash serum is known to help condition and enhance the natural look of lashes. Meghan told a magazine in 2014:

'I swear they are as long as they could ever be.'

Shu Uemura
Eyelash Curler

This curler is regarded as the best out there and Meghan told www.beautybanter.com that it's one of her top five must-haves, saying it:

'makes you look instantly awake.'

Fresh Sugar
Advanced Lip Treatment with SPF15

Meghan has said:

'I have searched high and low and tried every kind of lip balm but this is the very best. Soft, kissable, buttery lips – I swear by it.'

Charlotte Tilbury
'Very Victoria' Matte Revolution lipstick

British beauty brand Charlotte Tilbury makes one of Meghan's favourite lipsticks, according to 'Hello' magazine. The princess-to-be reportedly wore the 'Very Victoria' shade – a taupe nude matte – for her engagement day photos.

Tatcha
The Rice Polish Foaming Enzyme Powder

This water-activated exfoliant of Japanese rice bran transforms to a creamy foam and the Duchess has remarked that:

'it just sort of foams on your face and gives it a really subtle exfoliation.'

Bioré
Daily Deep Pore Cleansing Cloths

To keep her skin feeling fresh and clean, Meghan likes Bioré Daily Deep Poor Cleansing Cloths. She has said:

'They're great to keep in the car and on your nightstand when you have one of those horribly lazy nights when the thought of getting up to wash your face seems unbearable.'

Dr. Bronner's
Pure Castile Soap

Meghan uses Dr. Bronner's soap in lavender scent.

'I love the smell and it lasts for such a long time,' she has shared 'The almond scent is quite nice too if your prefer something warm and sweet. I alternate between the two.'

Nivea
Skin Firming Hydration Body Lotion

Meghan claims this affordable Nivea Skin Firming Hydration cream makes her skin look and feel amazing:

'I would buy a case of this at a time if I could find it.'

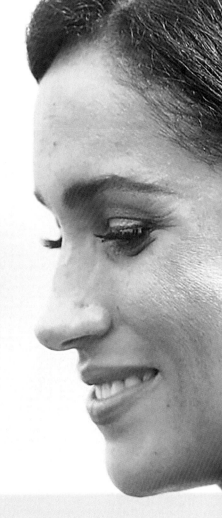

Wella
Oil Reflections Luminous Smoothing Oil

Meghan loves this smoothing hair oil by Wella. She told a beauty website.

'It smells like vacation and makes your hair slippery and touchable,' … 'I love this stuff! It also doubles as a pretty amazing body oil post-bath.'

Oribe
Dry Texturizing Spray

While Meghan was on set filming 'Suits', she frequently used Oribe Dry Texturizing spray. She said the trick is to bend forward, spray the dry shampoo, then:

'flip back hard' for 'a little extra bounce'.

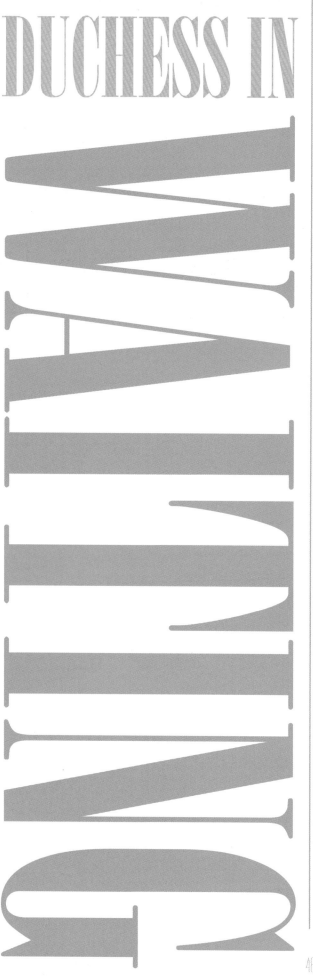

DUCHESS IN THE MAKING

'No one has owned this year more than Meghan Markle'

Harpers Bazaar

Meghan may have rocked a pair of artfully ripped *'First Fray'* jeans by LA-based company Mother Denim on her first appearance with Harry at the Invictus Games in Canada, but once she was engaged to a Prince and officially a Royal-in-waiting, she upped her style game and worked a *'modern-meets-royal'* aesthetic.

For the couple's first official joint engagement to Nottingham in early December 2017, Meghan's *'military-cut'* navy *'Elodie'* coat boasting large statement buttons was by Canadian label Mackage. She added a classic black roll-neck jumper by Wolford, a stylish nude midi skirt by Joseph, and a chic burgundy bag by Strathberry, completing her outfit with a pair of black boots by KG at Kurt Geiger. She wore her long black hair loosely around her shoulders and natural looking make-up. The *'Meghan Effect'* was off to a cracking start, with the coat and classic roll neck selling out just moments after she was seen wearing them.

For the Queen's pre-Christmas lunch for her extended family at Buckingham Palace later that month, we caught a glimpse of the Self-Portrait *'Nightshade'* midi dress and *'Snowflake'* earrings by her

Meghan Markle (handbag & boots detail) attends a Terrence Higgins Trust World AIDS Day charity fair at Nottingham Contemporary on December 1, 2017

favourite Canadian jeweller, Birk, which Meghan was wearing as she and Prince Harry drove through the Palace gates. However, on Christmas Day itself, Meghan and the rest of the Royal Family were photographed outside St Mary Magdalene Church, Sandringham and the Duchess-to-be's first festive fashion choices could be seen in all their glory. She rocked a bespoke Philip Treacy nutmeg brown velour beret hat with twist detail, a Sentaler wide-collar camel wrap coat, Stuart Weitzman *'Highland Boots'* in nutmeg suede, a Chloe *'Pixie'* small round handbag, and dark tan leather stitch-detail gloves from Marks and Spencer. The burgundy *'Tay'* velvet dress from Canadian clothes brand Club Monaco which she was wearing beneath her coat featured short, ruffled sleeves, a belted waist and cuts just below the knee. Taking to Instagram, a representative from Club Monaco said: *'A very short term #fbf to Christmas Day when we got a peek at the lovely @meghanmarkle wearing our velvet Tay dress to visit the royal family.'*

January 2018 dawned and in addition to planning her May 19 wedding, Meghan was back on walkabout as she and Harry attended a number of official engagements. Their first visit of the New Year was to youth radio station Reprezent 107.3FM in Brixton, South London. Meghan showed off her characteristically chic style in black Burberry wide-leg trousers with an Aritzia Amos dress belt, a black bell-sleeved sweater by Marks & Spencer – which sold out instantly, a Jigsaw *'Sara'* scarf, a Smythe *'Brando'* coat in camel, and Sarah Flint tortoiseshell heels. She accessorised her look with Birk Les Plaisirs de Birk gold earrings and a Zofia Day stack ring in 14k gold with pave diamonds. She sported trousers again on her next official visit - to Cardiff - a few weeks later, wearing high-waisted, *'Dina'* skinny fit black jeans by little known Welsh brand Huit Denim which were another instant sell-out, making it necessary for the company to instigate a three-month waiting list. Not surprisingly, the husband and wife team were delighted at Meghan's

Meghan Markle attends a Christmas Day church service at St Mary Magdalene on December 25, 2017 in King's Lynn, England

patronage. *'It's just a beautiful moment,'* they tweeted. *'There are things you hope for and wish for, but when they happen you think, "Wow"'* It's good for the team, it's good for the town and you go, *"Wow, we'll take that".'* To complete her *'Cardiff'* look, Meghan also wore a Stella McCartney tie detail coat in black, a Theory Hadfield plaid off-the-shoulder jacket, a DeNennellier London *'Mini Venice'* bag in forest green, Tabith Simmons *'KIKI'* black velvet boots and an Everlane black cashmere scarf. For her first visit to Edinburgh a month later, Meghan looked casually chic in a Burberry Double Breasted Tartan Wool Blend Coat and Veronica Beard *'Adley'* trousers in black.

In early February, Meghan and Harry made their first red carpet appearance at the Goldsmiths Hall in London for the Endeavour Fund Awards. But instead of wearing a traditional floor-length gown, Meghan opted for an edgier look, wearing an Alexander McQueen *'Grainde de Poudre'* wool blazer and straight-legged trousers, complete with Tuxe Bodywear *'The Boss'* bodysuit in silk crepe de chine, a Prada *'Biblioteque'* saffiano leather chain clutch bag, Manola Blanik BB black suede pointy-toed high-heeled pumps and Birk's gold bar earrings. It is rumoured that Meghan consulted Spice Girl turned fashion designer Victoria Beckham before this event. *'They get along well and have been in touch recently,'* a friend of the designer reportedly told a glossy fashion publication at this time. *'Meghan really likes Victoria's style and was keen to pick her brains about putting together a working wardrobe.'*

There was great excitement at the end of the month when Meghan and Harry appeared *'on stage'* for the first time with William and Kate at the Royal Foundation Forum in order to discuss the *'Heads Together'* charity. Meghan more than held her own in the style stakes, wearing a Jason Wu belted satin wrap dress in navy, uber-

Prince Harry and Meghan Markle walk through the corridors of the Palace of Holyrood house on their way to a reception for young people at the Palace on February 13, 2018 in Edinburgh, Scotland

fashionable Aquazzura *'Casablanca'* multistrap suede heels in black, and Isabel Marant enamelled gold tone hoop earrings, which were yet another instant sell-out.

For her next appearance for International Women's Day in Birmingham in early March, Meghan decided to mix chain store with designer. She sported a J Crew navy topped top coat and an All Saints *'Ridley'* chalk white sweater. Her black cropped trousers were Alexander Wang, her shoes the trusty Manola Blanik pumps and she carried a Althuzarra *'Giandra'* saddle bag in navy grain leather. Later in the month, Meghan attended her first official engagement with the Queen at Westminster Abbey for the Commonwealth Day Service. Looking majestically chic, the future Duchess wore a white/cream Crombie coat and midnight-blue *'Springstein'* midi dress by British fashion designer Amanda Wakeley, which she paired with a white/cream felt beret and the Mulberry *'Small Darley'* clutch bag in bright navy. On her feet were a navy version of her favourite Blanik, pointy-toed, high-heeled pumps.

In late March, Meghan and Harry made a surprise visit to Northern Ireland, where Meghan teamed a double-faced front drape wool coat by Mackage, with a green, flounce-hemmed skirt by Greta Constantine. She layered up in a cream cashmere sweater by Victoria Beckham and carried a Bloomsbury bag in chestnut from young British designer Charlotte Elizabeth. Jimmy Choo's *'Romy 100'* pumps in oxid-velvet finished the look.

April was a busy month. Before the first week was out, Meghan and Harry travelled to Bath to attend trials for the Invictus Games. She channelled a practical vibe in a Babaton *'Lawson'* trench coat, black Mother Denim boot-cut jeans and Stuart Weitzman *'Axiom'* ankle-boots. A few weeks later, the soon-to-be-marrieds visited the Commonwealth Youth Forum in London, with Meghan wearing a stunning *'Audrey'* pinstriped stretch-cotton trench dress from Altuzarra. She paired it with a black blazer from Australian label Camilla and Marc, a monochrome *'Avalon'* zip top crossbody from

Meghan Markle visits Millennium Point to attend an event celebrating International Women's Day on March 8, 2018 in Birmingham, England

Meghan Markle (handbag detail) attends a reception with delegates from the Commonwealth Youth Forum during the Commonwealth Heads of Government Meeting (CHOGM) at the Queen Elizabeth II Conference Centre on April 18, 2018 in London, England

Oroton, an Australian accessories brand, and Tamara Mellon *'Paramour'* shoes. The next night she attended a Commonwealth reception for women's empowerment and was dressed in a *'Jackie O'* LBD, inspired by the former FLOTUS. The dress featured an asymmetrical neckline and was cinched in at the waist with a leather belt. *'Even a royal-in-waiting can't resist the effortlessness of a little black dress,'* enthused Harpers Bazaar. Meghan accessorised with a Gucci black velvet mini Dionysus bag and Aquazzura *'Milano'* black suede pumps. On her ears were 18ct white and diamond orbs by Birk. For her next engagement – an Invictus Games Reception at Australia House – Meghan took a break from her mostly neutral Royal wardrobe and wore a bright green statement dress by Self-Portrait for the Invictus Games Sydney celebration. She paired it with her Alexander McQueen Grain de Poudre blazer, Roland Mouret bag, Cartier earrings, and Manolo Blahnik heels.

Her Majesty the Queen's 92nd Birthday Concert at London's Royal Opera House towards the end of the month required something extra special – a sophisticated evening look that combined fashion with formality. Meghan opted for a navy *'Stella'* by Stella McCartney cape dress and teamed with her navy Manolos. A Naeem Khan zodiac clutch bag and Shaun Leane *'Talon'* earrings completed the outfit.

Wedding fever was building, but there was still work of an official nature to do. The day after the birthday concert, Meghan – with Harry - attended a memorial service at St Martin-in-the-Fields, London, wearing a patterned sleeveless Hugo Boss midi dress and nude suede Manolos, carrying a Wilbur and Gussie bespoke Charlie Oyster silk clutch bag. She also wore her favourite Cartier white and gold *'Galanterie'* stud earrings. Next up was the early morning church service in London to commemorate Anzac Day. Meghan dressed for the occasion in a *'Pagoda'* grey coat by label Smythe, a large brimmed hat, black heels by Sarah Flint and her favourite Gucci Dionysus mini bag in velvet. Later that day for a service at Westminster Abbey, Meghan changed into a timeless bespoke Emilia Wickstead black, jacquard midi skirt and cropped matching jacket. She carried a black Jimmy Choo *'J Box'* clutch and wore her favourite black suede Manolos and Cartier studs.

As May dawned, wedding fever was building even more – but there was also trouble brewing of a family kind. Earlier in the month, it transpired that Meghan's father, Thomas, had set up and sold paparazzi photos of himself to the world's media. He then announced he was unable to attend his daughter's wedding due to emergency heart surgery. Meghan was reportedly devastated, but one wouldn't have known it to look at her on the eve of her wedding day. Having had tea with her mother, Doria, and soon-to-be grandmother-in-law, Queen Elizabeth II, Meghan positively glowed in a navy-coloured *'Barwick'* Roland Mouret dress with elegant Blanik light grey suede pumps on her feet. On her wrist hung a Bentley & Skinner diamond line bracelet – a gift from her father-in-law to be, Prince Charles.

Prince Harry and his US fiancée Meghan Markle leave after attending a memorial service at St Martin-in-the-Fields in Trafalgar Square in London, on April 23, 2018, to commemorate the 25th anniversary of the murder of Stephen Lawrence

ABOVE:

Meghan Markle attends an Invictus Games Reception at
Australia House on April 21, 2018 in London, England

RIGHT:

Meghan Markle attends an Anzac Day service at Westminster
Abbey on April 25, 2018 in London, England

TOTES AMAZING!

The Duchess of Sussex is the ultimate Royal bag lady. Every time she appears in public, she's carrying an exquisite piece of arm-candy and every piece she owns becomes an instant best seller – or even sell out. Here's a selection of the most memorable and style-savvy.

The Victoria Beckham Powder Box clutch bag

Complete with inner mirror – which Meghan
carried to church on Christmas Day 2018.

The Gabriela Hearst Nina bag.

Meghan sported the highly desirable GHN on her first visit to the county of Sussex in October 2018. Made in a unique sculptural shape, it unfurls at the top, opening to a smooth suede lining.

The DeMellier tote bag

The Duchess stepped out in Cardiff in January 2018 with this stunning forest green handbag by British leather goods company DeMellier.

The Mulberry Clifton shoulder bag

For a visit to London's Southbank Centre in July 2018, Meghan wowed fashionistas with this Rosewater design featuring a gold chain strap and striking button detail.

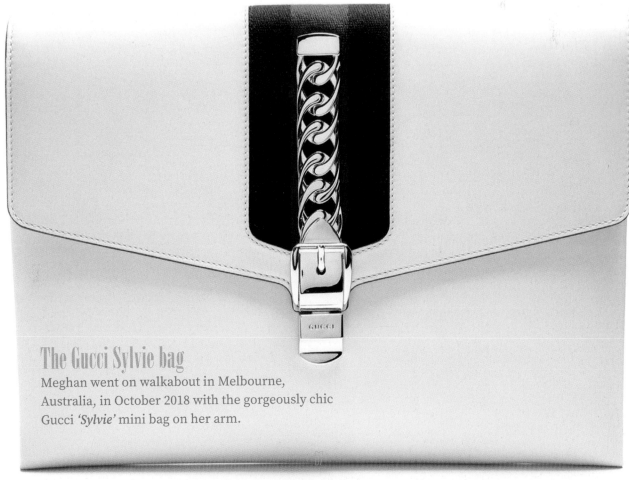

The Gucci Sylvie bag

Meghan went on walkabout in Melbourne, Australia, in October 2018 with the gorgeously chic Gucci *'Sylvie'* mini bag on her arm.

The Strathberry bags

A perennial favourite, Meghan is regularly seen sporting a Strathberry tote. She favoured a burgundy model of the Scottish label on her first official engagement with Prince Harry in Nottingham in late 2017. As a result, the bag sold out in minutes.

The Bloomsbury bag by Charlotte Elizabeth.

With modern curvatures inspired by classic cars, and a carry-top handle reminiscent of vintage ladies' handbags, the Duchess carried the Bloomsbury on a trip to Belfast in March 2018.

STRATHBERRY

The Everlane Cognac

Meghan was seen carrying the fabulous tan Everlane Cognac tote, crafted from Italian leather, when she attended the Invictus Games in Toronto with Prince Harry in September 2017.

The Celine bag

BH – ie, before Harry – Meghan was photographed in New York City in 2016 carrying a ghost white bag, by high-end designer Celine. Sleek, structured and eye-catching.

The Charlotte Olympia box clutch bag

In 2015, Meghan attended a high-profile fashion event for Vogue Magazine – The Fashion Fund Awards – and carried a pretty little transparent box clutch by British designer Charlotte Olympia.

The Roger Vivier Pilgrim de Jour bag

Meghan mixed up her business suit look for an appearance on the 'Today' show in the summer of 2016 with a pair of shorts, but still brought the business with her Roger Vivier Pilgrim de Jour bag!

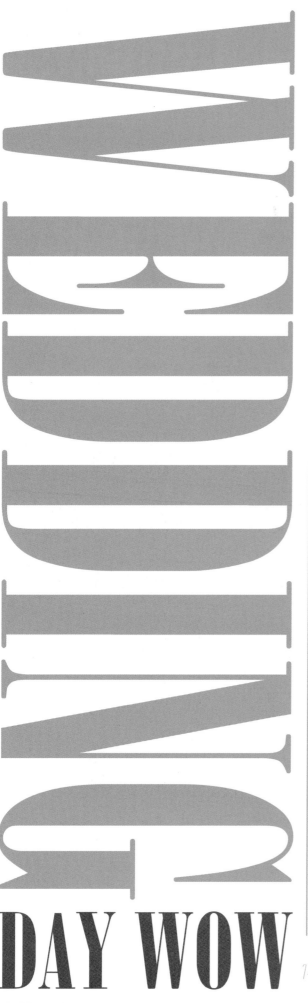

'A Perfect Fit'

Vogue magazine's verdict on Meghan's Givenchy-designed Wedding Gown

On May 19 2018 at 11.30 am precisely, Meghan and her mother Doria left the Cliveden House Hotel for St George's Chapel Windsor in a 1950 Rolls-Royce Phantom IV from the Queen's fleet – and the first glimpse of the future Duchess of Sussex in all her bridal finery was had.

Speculation about *'the dress'* was at fever pitch. What was it like? Who was the designer? Was it uber-glamorous Israeli designer Inbal Dror, who had revealed shortly after the engagement that he had been asked to submit designs for what would be the wedding dress of the decade? Turkish-Canadian designer Erdem Moralıoğlu? Edgy and innovative Stella McCartney? Sarah Burton of Alexander McQueen, designer of Kate Middleton's wedding dress? Departing creative director of Burberry Christopher Bailey, perhaps? Or was it the odds-on favourite? Husband and wife team Ralph & Russo who had designed Meghan's semi-sheer black evening dress for her official engagement portrait and whose haute couture atelier team had been seen visiting the Royal School of Needlework. In the event it turned out to be none of these.

As Meghan stepped out of the Rolls, a vision in ice-white silk, Kensington Palace tweeted that the designer was Clare Waight

Meghan Markle and her mother, Doria Ragland arrive at Cliveden House Hotel on the National Trust's Cliveden Estate to spend the night before her wedding to Prince Harry on May 18, 2018

Meghan Markle arrives at St George's Chapel at Windsor
Castle for her wedding to Prince Harry on May 19, 2018
in Windsor, England

Keller of Givenchy, British-born Artistic Director of the iconic Parisian fashion house that had famously dressed Audrey Hepburn and was reknowned for its classically chic, stylish designs.

The wedding dress was simple – minimalist even – without lace or any other embellishment. It featured slim, three-quarter-lengthed sleeves and an open-boat neckline which graciously framed the shoulders and emphasized Meghan's slender waist. A built-in train was draped in soft folds over a triple silk organza underskirt. Comprising just six seams, the gown was made from double-bonded silk cady, sourced after extensive research across Europe, giving it an intense, Block-white colour. Contemporary in design it may have been, but the gown made Meghan look nothing less than a fairytale princess. Romantically, a piece of the blue dress from her first date with Prince Harry was stitched into the lining.

The 16-foot veil of soft ivory silk tulle was a work of art on its own, embroidered specifically with the signature flowers of all 53 countries in the British Commonwealth. Wintersweet, found in Kensington Palace Gardens, and the California poppy, in commemoration of Meghan's birthplace, were two further floral additions. Painstakingly researched by Waight Keller, the inclusion of the flowers was a surprise for Prince Harry, in a nod to his role as Commonwealth Youth Ambassador.

'Harry was really over the moon to find out that I would make this choice for our day together,' Meghan was later to say.

So why, of all the top designers in the world, had Meghan chosen the House of Givenchy? It seems she didn't begin to plan her dress until a month after her engagement. In December 2017, her best friend and bridal expert Jessica Mulroney told the bride-to-be that the search for a Royal wedding dress designer needed to begin immediately. Meghan knew exactly what she was looking for – a dress that was modern yet elegant, timeless and appropriate. With the help of Mulroney, she worked her way through a list of potential designers – including Burberry, Ralph & Russo, Erdem and Stella McCartney. However, one name emerged as favourite – Givenchy.

Prince Harry, Duke of Sussex and the Duchess of Sussex kiss as they leave St George's Chapel, Windsor Castle after their wedding ceremony on May 19, 2018 in Windsor, England

While a French couture house may not have been the most obvious choice, creative Clare Waight Keller ticked the most important box – she was British. Born in Birmingham in the west Midlands, she could fly the flag for British fashion at the wedding of the decade.

'I think she had seen my work and knew what I did,' Waight Keller later said. 'I think she loved the fact that I was a British designer and working in a house such as Givenchy, which has its roots in a classical, beautiful style from the time of Hubert de Givenchy himself. It was an extraordinary moment when she told me she wanted me to design the dress. It was an incredible thing to be part of, such an historic moment, and to have the opportunity to work with her – it was a wonderful way to start the collaboration with her.'

In the following weeks, sketches went back and forth between Meghan and her designer, with the pair establishing a fast friendship through texts, phone calls and brief meetings.

'From the very start we had a few variations on the design, but then very quickly it held to the final creation that you saw,' Waight Keller revealed.

In mid-February, Meghan secretly visited the designer at a location in south-west London to look at an archive of designs and pieces from her work with Chloé and Pringle of Scotland, sketches and catalogues from the House of Givenchy and an array of fabric samples and archival runway looks.

'She was really focused, as I was, on it being absolutely perfect for the occasion,' said Waight Keller. 'And also knowing what the House of Givenchy has done in its history. I think it was a collaboration that came through that. We exchanged conversations about what would be the ultimate lines and proportions and the scale of the dress, but over time we got to a point where I knew that she knew exactly what she wanted, having tried some of the toiles and mock-ups that I had shown her. And then it evolved into the final design.'

Two small teams—the members of which all signed nondisclosure agreements – set up a private workspace at the Givenchy Haute Couture Atelier in Paris and an undisclosed workshop location in London. The silk tulle veil took longer to complete than the dress, with almost 500 hours meticulously spent creating each flower with silk threads and organza on a flat surface before sewing it onto the

The Duchess of Sussex departs after her wedding to Prince Harry, Duke of Sussex at St George's Chapel, Windsor Castle on May 19, 2018 in Windsor, England

veil. It was so delicate, the embroiderers had to wash their hands every 30 minutes to keep the tulle and threads clean.

With work taking place in two different workshops – one for the dress, another for the veil – it wasn't until early April that the near-complete design was united in London, ready for what turned into three further in-person fittings to get the soft silhouette just right. In May, the finished article was quietly transported to Windsor Castle, where it was safely stored until Meghan – joined by Jessica Mulroney – could attend one final fitting.

'There were a few adjustments in the later fittings, but by the time we got to the third stage, we were quite close to knowing what we needed to do,' Waight Keller explained.

There was just one last person who needed to see it – the Queen. Just like the Duchess of Cambridge did three weeks before marrying Prince William in 2011, Meghan privately presented a first look at the finished gown to Her Majesty before the big day – not exactly for approval but to share a special moment with her grandmother-in-law to be.

On the day itself, as the delicate white floral embroidery of Meghan's almost translucent veil caught the light as she elegantly glided down the aisle of St. George's Chapel towards Harry, Clare Waight Keller felt a moment of immense pride for what had been five months of love and labour.

'She was just glowing,' the designer recalls. *'I was just thrilled to be part of it. It was a wonderful moment for both of them and I am really proud.'*

As was Prince Harry.

'Oh my God, thank you,' he said to Waight Keller as he and his new wife posed for photographs in Windsor Castle's Green Drawing Room. *'She looks absolutely stunning.'*

US actress Meghan Markle arrives for the wedding ceremony to marry Britain's Prince Harry, Duke of Sussex, at St George's Chapel, Windsor Castle, in Windsor, on May 19, 2018

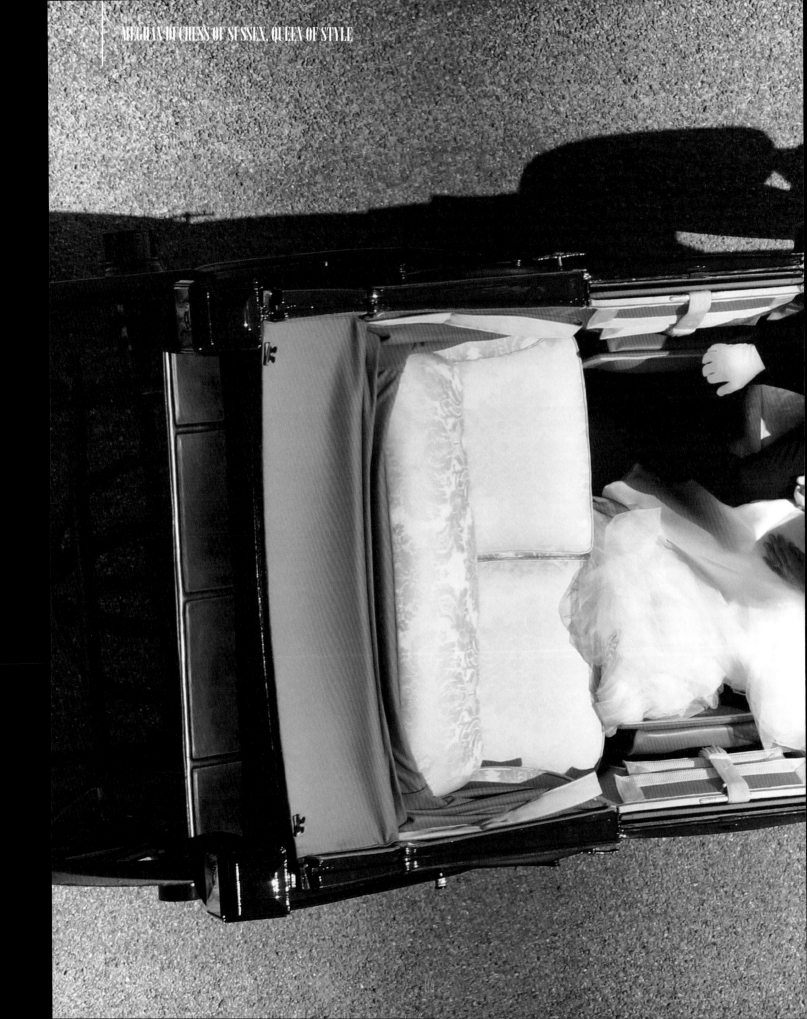

Prince Harry, Duke of Sussex and his wife Meghan, Duchess of Sussex ride in the Ascot Landau Carriage as they pass through Cambridge Gate into the grounds of Windsor Castle

Duchess of Sussex and Prince Harry, Duke of Sussex leave Windsor Castle after their wedding to attend an evening reception at Frogmore House, hosted by the Prince of Wales on May 19, 2018 in Windsor, England.

THE ACCESSORIES

Shoes

To complement the gown, Meghan's high-heeled wedding shoes were based on the Givenchy refined pointed SS18 Haute Couture design made of a silk duchess satin. These were visible as she emerged from the Rolls before ascending the steps of St George's Chapel.

All that Glitters

Meghan is a long-term lover of delicate jewellery and on her wedding day, she didn't disappoint. In addition to her diamond engagement ring, she wore diamond earrings by Cartier – elegant and refined, just like the bride. On her left wrist she wore a matching Cartier bracelet. Her wedding ring was hewn from rare Welsh gold. Royal brides have historically been given wedding rings made from the golden nuggets of Clogau St David's mine at Bontddu, north Wales – a tradition which goes back 88 years.

Almost every royal bride in history has worn a tiara on her wedding day, and Meghan was no exception. She accessorised her stunning veil with the dazzling, glittering Queen Mary Diamond Bandeau tiara, loaned by the Queen. The Queen Mary Diamond Bandeau tiara is a little-known piece which was first created for the Queen's grandmother, Queen Mary, back in 1932. It features a detachable brooch, given to Mary as a wedding present in 1893 by the County of Lincoln. The beautiful tiara features a stunning floral-shaped suspended brooch in the centre made of one large round diamond and surrounded by nine smaller diamonds. The bandeau part of the tiara contains 11 intricate, glittering sections, including ovals and pavé set with large and small diamonds. Queen Mary bequeathed the bandeau and brooch to the Queen on her death in 1953.

Flower Power

Prince Harry handpicked several flowers from his and Meghan's private garden at Kensington Palace to add to the bespoke bridal bouquet, designed by florist Philippa Craddock. It included forget-me-nots which were Diana, Princess of Wales' favourite flower and were specifically chosen to honour the memory of the late princess. The small bouquet also featured scented sweet peas, lily of the valley, astilbe, jasmine and astrantia and the traditional sprigs of myrtle, all bound with a naturally dyed raw silk ribbon. London-based florist Ms Craddock also created the floral displays at the chapel, which were filled with white garden roses, peonies and foxgloves, branches of beech, birch and hornbeam.

Wedding Hair and Make-up

Meghan Markle didn't disappoint in the beauty stakes at her wedding.

Her make-up was impossibly fresh and glowing, thanks to Christian Dior make-up artist, Daniel Martin who gave her that natural yet illusive, lit-from-within look. A light, subtle base was added to her already flawless skin, leaving her freckles on display. She opted for a subtle, smokey eyeshadow with a smattering of mascara. A sheer, pink lip gloss was added to her lips, adding to her all-over radiant glow. Her nails complemented the whole look perfectly; the shape was simple – short and round and the colour, a pinky-nude, didn't overshadow her engagement and wedding rings. The former actress opted to wear her glossy, long hair in a bun, styled by Serge Normant, who also works with the likes of actress Sarah Jessica Parker.

Prince Harry, Duke of Sussex and his wife Meghan, Duchess of Sussex leave from the West Door of St George's Chapel, Windsor Castle, in Windsor on May 19, 2018 in Windsor, England

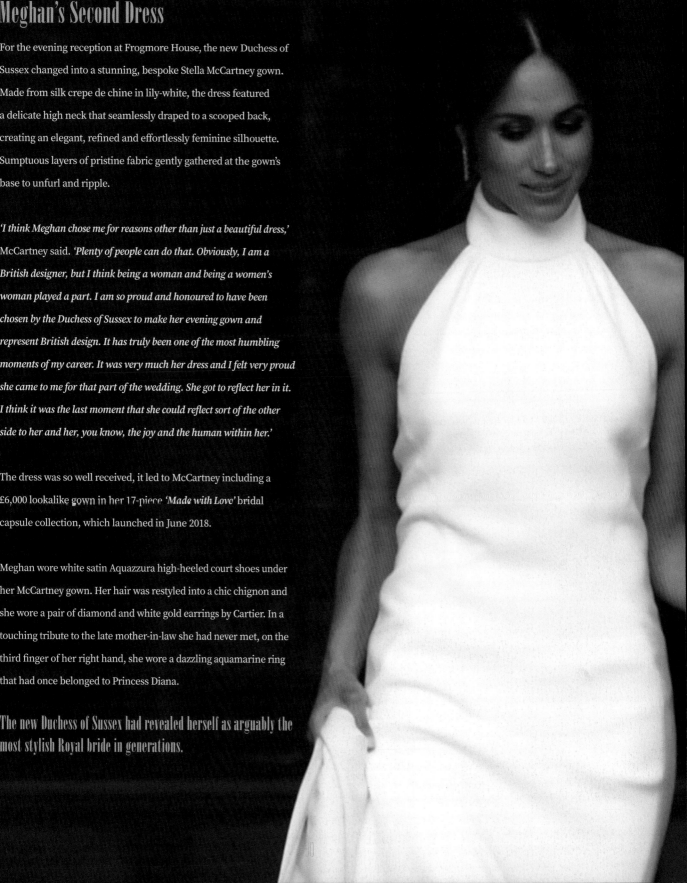

Meghan's Second Dress

For the evening reception at Frogmore House, the new Duchess of Sussex changed into a stunning, bespoke Stella McCartney gown. Made from silk crepe de chine in lily-white, the dress featured a delicate high neck that seamlessly draped to a scooped back, creating an elegant, refined and effortlessly feminine silhouette. Sumptuous layers of pristine fabric gently gathered at the gown's base to unfurl and ripple.

'I think Meghan chose me for reasons other than just a beautiful dress,' McCartney said. *'Plenty of people can do that. Obviously, I am a British designer, but I think being a woman and being a women's woman played a part. I am so proud and honoured to have been chosen by the Duchess of Sussex to make her evening gown and represent British design. It has truly been one of the most humbling moments of my career. It was very much her dress and I felt very proud she came to me for that part of the wedding. She got to reflect her in it. I think it was the last moment that she could reflect sort of the other side to her and her, you know, the joy and the human within her.'*

The dress was so well received, it led to McCartney including a £6,000 lookalike gown in her 17-piece *'Made with Love'* bridal capsule collection, which launched in June 2018.

Meghan wore white satin Aquazzura high-heeled court shoes under her McCartney gown. Her hair was restyled into a chic chignon and she wore a pair of diamond and white gold earrings by Cartier. In a touching tribute to the late mother-in-law she had never met, on the third finger of her right hand, she wore a dazzling aquamarine ring that had once belonged to Princess Diana.

The new Duchess of Sussex had revealed herself as arguably the most stylish Royal bride in generations.

Duchess of Sussex and Prince Harry, Duke of Sussex leave Windsor Castle after their wedding to attend an evening reception at Frogmore House, hosted by the Prince of Wales, on May 19, 2018 in Windsor, England

MEGHAN ON THE HIGH STREET

While she loves haute couture and top-drawer designers, Meghan also mixes up her look with chain store items. Here are some of the most accessible.

J Crew

Black Excursion Quilted Down Vest

Navy Tipped Topcoat

'Sadie' Black Suede Ankleboots

'Toothpick' Jeans in Charcoal Wash

Fan Rattan Clutch Bag

Field Mechanic jacket (Pictured)

Marks & Spencer

Wool Blend Bell Sleeve Sweater in Black (Pictured)

M&S Collection Pillbox Bow Fascinator in Cream

Leather Stitch Gloves

H&M

'Mama' Fine Knit Dress in Beige Melange (Pictured)

'Mama' Boyfriend Jean

And Other Stories

Polka-dot Waist Knot Midi Dress

Dark Green Straight-Fit Silk Shirt (Pictured)

All Saints

Ridley Chalk White Sweater (Pictured)

ASOS

Maternity *'Wiggle'* Mini Dress (Pictured)

Banana Republic

Madison 12 Hour Suede Cut-Out Pump in Blue

Graphite (Pictured)

Seasalt

'Lagoon' Navy Rain Jacket (Pictured)

Veja

V-10 White and Black Trainers (Pictured)

Jigsaw

'Sara' Scarf

Adidas

'Super Nova' Ink Blue 7/8 Tights

Nike

Classic Cortez Sneakers

HRH THE DUCHESS OF SUSSEX

'A Designer's Dream'

ABC News, Australia

There was no honeymoon period for the new Duke and Duchess of Sussex, at least not in the geographical sense. Four days after their Windsor wedding, they made their first official appearance as a married couple, stepping out to celebrate the 70th birthday of Prince Charles at a Buckingham Palace Garden Party. Meghan looked suitably demure and Royal Duchess-like in a rose-hued dress from Goat, paired with a matching Philip Treacy hat, a Wilbur and Gussie oyster silk clutch bag and Tamara Mellon *'Siren'* leather high-heeled pumps. Gone was her signature messy bun and predisposition for little-known, cool fashion brands, and in their place a sleek chignon, a traditional modest dress by a Duchess of Cambridge-approved label and a formal hat. She also wore tights on her slender legs – which the Queen may have approved of but Meghan fans definitely did not. *'I really hope that now Meghan Markle is officially Royal her style continues. Looking at her outfit, it was pretty, yet conservative and kind of made her blend in to the masses. But more importantly… who dressed her in tights that are paler than her own skin tone?!'* questioned one tweet.

Prince Harry and Meghan, Duchess of Sussex return in a horse-drawn carriage after attending the Queen's Birthday Parade, Trooping the Colour on Horse Guards Parade in London on June 9, 2018

However, Meghan raised establishment eyebrows at the Trooping of the Colour and during her first appearance on the Buckingham Palace Balcony for the traditional RAF flypast in honour of the Queen's official birthday in early June. She wore a bespoke Carolina Herrara off-the-shoulder portrait collar top and midi pencil skirt in baby pink. Off-the-shoulder? For a formal, daytime Royal occasion? It was simply not done – or hadn't been until now. Meghan's outfit broke with the Royal tradition of wearing more conservative necklines, particularly at Trooping the Colour. Not even that Royal fashion icon, the late Princess Diana, had ventured beyond long sleeves territory at the Queen's grand birthday celebration. However, Meghan abided by Royal protocol for Ascot, channelling her bridal look in another white dress by Givenchy. This one featured shirt-style centre buttons and a black belt, which she matched with Balenciaga heels and a monochrome Philip Treacy hat. Meghan opted for Givenchy again while undertaking her first solo engagement with the Queen in Cheshire. She accessorised a bespoke cream sheath dress with detachable capelet with a

Givenchy belt in black, a Givenchy black triple crossbody bag and black Sarah Flint 100' *'Perfect Pumps'*.

Continuing her neutral-wardrobe theme, Meghan opted for a pale pink skirt suit with asymmetrical draped hem by Prada when she joined Prince Harry and the Queen to meet *the winners of the Queen's Young Leaders Awards* at Buckingham Palace in late June 2018. However, for her next two formal engagements, she embraced colour. Meghan stepped out in a sunshine yellow, boat-necked sheath dress by Lady Gaga's stylist Brandon Maxwell when she and Prince Harry met Commonwealth youth leaders at London's Marlborough House that July. Four days later, for Prince Louis' christening, Aunt Meghan was dressed in a bespoke olive-green Ralph Lauren dolman-sleeved dress with boat-neck and belted waist, and a bespoke Stephen Jones sheer hat in olive green. Her final engagement before embarking on her first overseas trip as a Royal Duchess to Ireland was at a thanksgiving service for the RAF at Westminster Abbey. For this she donned a haute-couture,

Meghan Markle attends an Anzac Day Service of Commemoration and Thanksgiving at Westminster Abbey on April 25, 2018 in London

midnight-hued fit-and-flare Dior dress, Stephen Jones custom-made navy crinoline propeller fascinator, Dior *'D-choc'* nude high-heeled pumps and a Dior navy satin clutch bag. She also sported her favourite Cartier Galantine earrings.

On arrival in Dublin on July 10 2018, Meghan was wearing an appropriately *'Irish-green'* pencil skirt and matching crewneck knit top by Givenchy, Paul Andrew *'Pump-It Up'* tan suede pumps with toe cap detail and a Strathberry midi tote-bag in tan. She continued the Irish theme by sporting Vanessa Tugendhaft *'Precious Clover'* charm stud earrings. For a summer garden party at the British Ambassador's Residence in Dublin that evening, Meghan shone in a chic black midi cocktail dress by Emilia Wickstead, Aquarazza *'Deneuvre'* heels, a Givenchy clutch bag and Morganite drop earrings from Birks. For her third *'Irish'* outfit, she wore a grey taupe Roland Mouret dress accessorised with Paul Andrew *'Pump It Up'* black heels and a Fendi *'Peekaboo'* bag in black calfskin leather.

Once back in the UK, Meghan wowed crowds at Wimbledon when she arrived to watch the Women's Final wearing a striped shirt and white trousers by Ralph Lauren. Other standout looks from summer/autumn 2018 include a pink trench coat dress by the Canadian brand House of Nonie, combined with a Mulberry clutch and blush Dior heels, which she wore to London's Southbank Centre; a denim Carolina Herrera dress with a J Crew wicker bag, Michael Kors sunglasses, and nude Aquazzura heels worn to watch the Duke of Sussex play in the Sentebale Polo Cup; a black wool tuxedo dress by Judith & Charles with Shaun Leane earrings and Paul Andrew heels to a charitable performance of 'Hamilton' in London; a blue bespoke Jason Wu dress with a Dior clutch and Aquazzura satin heels to the 100 Days to Peace charity gala at Westminster's Central Hall; a coat by Smythe and a black skirt by Misha Nonoo for the launch of *'Together: Our Community Cookbook'*

Meghan, Duchess of Sussex arrives at Dublin airport at the start of a two day visit to Ireland on July 10, 2018

Meghan, Duchess of Sussex poses during a Welcome Event at Admiralty House on October 16, 2018 in Sydney, Australia

at Kensington Palace; an olive-green Hugo Boss leather skirt teamed with And Other Stories shirt; and a bespoke navy funnel-neck coat and matching dress by Givenchy, Noel Stewart navy straw beret hat, and Manolo navy heels at the October wedding of Princess Eugenie.

Meghan announced her pregnancy on October 15, the first day of her and Harry's 16-day visit to New Zealand, Fiji, Tonga and Australia. A marathon of a tour involving 76 engagements, all eyes were on the Duchess' fashion choices.

For their first day in Sydney, Meghan arrived at Admiralty House in a simple white shift dress. Following the Royal baby news, the classic number was aptly called the *'Blessed Dress'* and also paid homage to their host country as it was by Australian designer Karen

Gee. Touchingly, Meghan chose to accessorise the ensemble with butterfly earrings and a bracelet which had belonged to the late Princess Diana. Their next stops, which included a trip to Taronga Zoo, as well as meeting members of the public outside the Opera House, saw Meghan wrap up in a beige trench coat by Melbourne-born designer Martin Grant – changing for the afternoon reception into a forest green button-up dress with pleated skirt by Brandon Maxwell.

For their second day, which saw the couple take a trip to Dubbo, Meghan opted for a more dressed-down ensemble, pairing black skinny jeans with a white oversized shirt and checked blazer. The trendy number was designed by her good friend, tennis champion Serena Williams. Meanwhile, her black jeans were by Aussie brand Outland Denim, created by James Bartle to help survivors of sex

and human trafficking in Cambodia. Meghan also complemented her relaxed look with a simple low ponytail.

On day three, Meghan wore two chic dresses for a trip to Melbourne. The first, a striking royal blue dress by yet another Australian designer, Dion Lee. In the afternoon, the couple then made a quick stop at Melbourne Beach, where she changed into a black dress with gold-tone buttons by Club Monaco. She covered up throughout the day once again in the beige trench coat by Martin Grant and, upon hitting the beach, sensibly changed out of her Manolos into a pair of sustainable Rothy's shoes

Meghan arrived at Sydney's famous Bondi Beach on day four in a statement striped maxi dress by Australian designer Martin Grant. She paired the dress, from the designer's Resort 2019 collection, with a pair of wedged espadrilles by Spanish brand Castaner

For the afternoon activities – a visit to Macarthur Girls High School before meetings with Australian dignitaries – Meghan upped her style, changing into a two-tone blue dress by British brand Roksanda. She subtly accessorised the elegant A-line dress with blue topaz earrings, which were highlighted by her half-up half-down hairstyle and a slim silver bracelet, both by Meghan's go-to Canadian jewellers, Birks. For the opening of the refurbished Anzac memorial the next day, Meghan wore a chic button-up black dress by British designer, Emilia Wickstead, accessorising with a Philip Treacy fascinator and Givenchy satin clutch. Later in the day she opted for a more casual look for the first day of the Invictus Games – a pair of Mother Denim black skinny jeans, an Invictus Games shirt and white Altuzarra blazer. She also sported a pair of statement tortoiseshell sunglasses by New York brand Illesteva and black heels by Tabitha Simmons. Day five also saw the couple attend the Invictus Games opening ceremony, Meghan changing into a Stella McCartney dress and

Meghan, Duchess of Sussex takes a tour of Anzac Memorial in Hyde Park, on October 20, 2018 in Sydney, Australia

matching navy coat by actress Gillian Anderson's first fashion line for Winser London. Remaining in Sydney on day six, Meghan cut a more casual figure than normal, sporting a pair of black skinny jeans with a turtleneck jumper by Australian brand Wolford and pinstripe blazer by L'Agence for a reception hosted by the Prime Minister of Australia. Her black and white stripe crossbody bag by Australian designer Oroton was a throwback to her 'Suits' days. To watch the final of the Invictus Games sailing competition, Meghan ditched her blazer for an an Invictus Games jacket designed by Superdry, paired with trendy Veja trainers.

On day seven, Meghan arrived on Queensland's Fraser Island in a maroon polka-dot dress by And Other Stories. For a later walkabout, she wore a striped, white and grey linen summer dress by popular Instagram brand Reformation – pairing it with Sarah Flint sandals and Karen Walker sunglasses. Arriving at Fiji airport on the eighth day of the tour, Meghan stepped off the plane looking elegant in white ensemble consisting of a simple white midi dress by Australian brand Zimmerman and hat by British milliner Stephen Jones. She accessorised the look with pearl drop earrings gifted to her by the Queen and a bracelet given to her by Prince Charles. That evening, Meghan att

Prince Harry, Duke of Sussex and Meghan, Duchess of Sussex arrive at the Sydney Opera House on October 16, 2018 in Sydney, Australia. The Duke and Duchess of Sussex are on their official 16-day autumn tour visiting cities in Australia, Fiji, Tonga and New Zealand

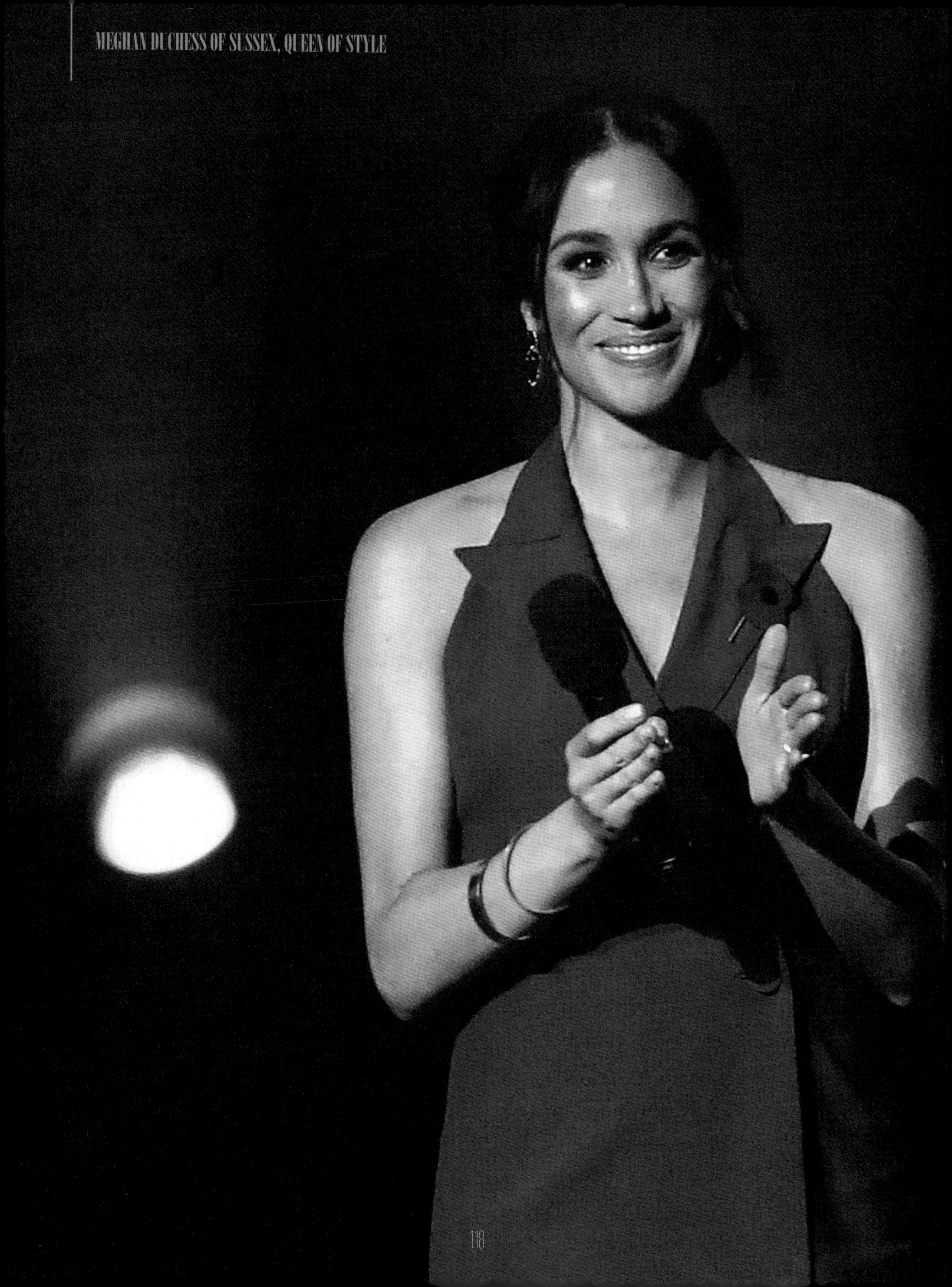

her first state dinner in an elegant caped gown by London-based brand Safiya, pairing it with diamond earrings thought to have been borrowed from Her Majesty's collection. To visit a local Fijian market on day nine, Meghan wore a bohemian, floral dress – complete with pompom tassels – by Figue. She carried a clutch bag which had been sourced from the local Suva market and debuted a beautiful floral updo adorned with fresh frangipani flowers. For their final engagement in Fiji, Meghan wore a forest-green sheath dress by Jason Wu. She accessorised with delicate gold jewellery, including two bangles and dainty gold leaf earrings. The Royal couple then flew on to Tonga, where Meghan stepped off the plane in a striking red outfit which was a modified version of a dress by London label, Self-Portrait. Later, Meghan wore her third outfit of the day – a glamorous evening gown by Theia, a New York brand beloved by Khloe Kardashian and Taylor Swift. She accessorised the look with a Givenchy clutch and Princess Diana's aquamarine ring. For her second day on Tonga, Meghan wore a khaki-striped cotton shirt dress by Australian Martin Grant. She later changed into a sky-blue dress in a similar style by Veronica Beard. Throughout the day, her hair was

styled, once again, into a sleek ponytail with her make-up kept very neutral. That evening, following a flight back to Sydney to attend an awards ceremony, Meghan stunned in an exquisite Oscar de la Renta cocktail dress with delicate tulle skirt featuring appliqué detail.

For the close of the Invictus Games, Meghan wore a Scanlan Theodore jacket with black jeans, accessorising her look with Sarah Flint heels and Shaun Leane earrings. That evening, Meghan spoke at the 2018 Invictus Games Closing Ceremony, wearing an olive-green Antonio Berardi tuxedo-style dress with nude heels. The Duchess wore her hair in her signature messy low bun. For her Sydney departure on day 13, the Duchess of Sussex paired a burgundy Hugo Boss dress with a nude shoes by Aquazzura and bag by Cuyana. For a walkabout in Wellington, New Zealand, Meghan wore an ASOS maternity dress under a checked trench coat by New Zealand designer Karen Walker. She accessorised the look with Muse Citrine Diamond earrings by her favourite jeweller, Birks. Meghan wore a custom Gabriela Hearst dress to an evening reception at Goverment House, with a Dior clutch, Stuart Weitzman heels and Maori design necklace.

Remaining in Wellington on Day 14, Meghan wore her Outland jeans which she had debuted in Dubbo again, a black sweater by Australian brand Jac + Jack, a khaki trench coat by Club Monaco and statement black ankle boots by Stuart Weitzman. That afternoon, for a visit to Abel Tasman National Park, Meghan sported a waterproof jacket by British brand Seasalt Cornwall, which she paired once again with her Outland jeans and a pair of trendy sustainable Stan Smith trainers by Stella McCartney. For the evening event, Meghan wore a white blazer dress by Maggie Marilyn, an ethically made brand in New Zealand. In Auckland on day 15, Meghan paired an off-white dress by Brandon Maxwell with a classic trench coat by British brand Burberry. Her second outfit of the day was a pair of J Crew skinny jeans and a coordinating navy blazer by Karen Walker. The Duchess then dressed up for an evening reception at the Auckland War Memorial, wearing a navy waterfall dress with button detail by Antonio Berardi

On the final day of the tour, the Duke and Duchess visited Rotorua, where Meghan wore an asymmetrical dress in midnight blue that had been custom made by Stella McCartney.

At Te Papaiouru Marae, she was gifted a woven Korowai, a Māori cloak said to give her strength during her pregnancy. She accessorised the look with a Pounamu Kouma necklace made by leading Māori designer Kiri Nathan. Later that day Meghan changed into a cobalt blue pleated skirt and matching jumper by Givenchy, which she paired with Manolo Blahnik heels. For their final 76th engagement to Redwoods Forest, Meghan sported a pair of black skinny jeans with a puffer jacket by Norrona which is thought to have belonged to her husband.

The fashion world's verdict on the tour?
'A Designer's Dream,'
according to Australia's ABC News.

Meghan, Duchess of Sussex visits the newly unveiled UK war memorial and Pukeahu National War Memorial Park on October 28, 2018 in Wellington, New Zealand

ABOVE:

Meghan, Duchess of Sussex arrives to open 'Oceania' at the Royal Academy of Arts on September 25, 2018 in London, England

OPP PAGE L:

Meghan, Duchess of Sussex visits The Nelson Mandela Centenary Exhibition at the Southbank Centre on July 17, 2018 in London, England

OPP PAGE R:

Meghan, The Duchess of Sussex seen during her visit to Ireland at Áras an Uachtaráin on July 11, 2018 in Dublin, Ireland

HOW MEGHAN
IS MAKING HER OWN ROYAL

STYLE RULES

Bare-legged Lady

Until Meghan, no Royal lady ever pitched up for an official engagement or photo call barelegged – not even in the height of summer. But this wife of a Prince was determined to lose the panty hose from the start. She went barelegged for the official engagement photo call in November 2017 and has done so on many occasions since – even though the Queen is said to disapprove. When Meghan does do hosiery – such as at the Buckingham Palace Garden Party in celebration of Prince Charles' 70th birthday - the tights never looks quite right.

Nailing It!

It's said that Elizabeth II finds coloured finger nails rather vulgar, which explains why Her Majesty has only worn Essie's neutral Ballet Slippers shade for years and why the Duchess of Cambridge is only ever seen sporting a natural-looking manicure. The Duchess of Sussex, however, broke with this protocol when she arrived at the Fashion Design Awards in London in late 2018 with her nails painted a distinctly dark hue.

Sheer Style

Even Meghan and Harry's engagement photos were a deviation from royal fashion protocol. For shots that were more high-end glossy magazine than House of Windsor, Meghan chose to wear a stunning sheer dress by Ralph and Russo. While the gown was still respectfully demure, the transparent material was certainly a break from tradition.

Hats Off!

According to the British press, the Duchess ruffled a few feathers during her first solo trip with Queen Elizabeth II by not wearing a hat. As Her Majesty had accessorised her outfit with a headpiece, it was understood that Meghan would follow suit – but she didn't. Conversely when Meghan took a Fedora to wear at the Wimbledon tennis championships, she was not allowed to sport it in the Royal Box.

Wearing the trousers

While it's said that Queen Elizabeth II prefers women in the family to choose dresses and skirts for official appearances, Meghan opted for a pair of white trousers and a striped shirt from Ralph Lauren for Wimbledon. The Duchess is also fond of a perfectly tailored trouser suit – such as the Alexander McQueen two-piece she wore to a charity awards event on her first official evening engagement with her Prince.

Getting Messy

The former Ms Markle is famous for wearing her hair in a *'messy bun'* – a style no other Royal lady has ever chosen, or dared to, adopt. Blue-blooded *'up-does'* are traditionally neat with not a hair out of place. For a while after her marriage, Royal protocol kicked in and Meghan's *up-does* tended to be of the sleek-backed chignon variety. But thankfully, now *'the messy'* is back.

Crossbody Bag

Meghan raised eyebrows when she accessorised with a Strathberry crossbody bag in bottle green rather than the usual clutch on a visit to Edinburgh Castle. According to etiquette expert William Hanson, *'It is protocol that you do not extend your hand to any member of the Royal family (blood Royal or those who have married into the family) unless their hand extends first.'* Meghan's CBB left her hands free to accept handshakes and presents from well wishers in Scotland.

Five, or More, Gold Rings

Royal wives traditionally sport just wedding and engagements rings on the third finger of their left hands – but not Meghan. On her right thumb, she regularly wears a gold ring by Turkish brand Kismet featuring the outline of a hand containing an eye with a blue sapphire. Known as a *'hamsa'*, the symbol is said to bring the wearer good fortune, happiness and health. She also enjoys wearing a perfectly mismatched selection of stacked rings by brands like Catbird and Baublebar on her right hand. *'Meghan has worn her stacking rings for many years now, long before she met Prince Harry,'* says Royal fashion blogger Susan Courter. *'I don't ever recall Kate or another Royal wearing similar rings, so it is certainly unique in regards to royal fashion. This is Meghan's way of injecting some of her personal style into Royal fashion. I think it's another way for her to show how you can still be yourself, keep a bit of that fashion flair.'*

Back in Black

The Queen reportedly prefers family members to wear black only when they're in mourning. However, her grand daughter-in-law has worn the darkest hue on several occasions such as the little black dress she sported at a reception for Women's Empowerment in London, the bespoke Givenchy one-shouldered velvet column gown she wore while pregnant at the Fashion Council Awards, and the sleeveless black Emilia Wickstead dress she wore in Ireland.

Footloose

Royals are expected to keep their shoes on at all times – even when walking on a beach. Think Kate Middleton, who reportedly kept her shoes on at Manly Beach, Australia in 2014, and Princess Diana, who did the same at New South Wales Beach in Terrigal in 1983. Not our Meghan, though. She ditched her Castaner espadrille wedges at Bondi Beach during a tour with Prince Harry in October 2018. She was kicking back already by wearing wedges – allegedly the Queen dislikes the style.

Off-the-Shoulder

'Fashion tradition usually dictates that Royal women do not wear off-the-shoulder or other more revealing styles,' a British newspaper wrote the day after the new Duchess of Sussex made her Buckingham balcony debut on June 9 2018 in celebration of Queen Elizabeth's birthday. Meghan clearly didn't get the memo – or she chose to ignore it – and wore a stunning, *'off-the-shoulder'* number in pale pink from Carolina Herrera.

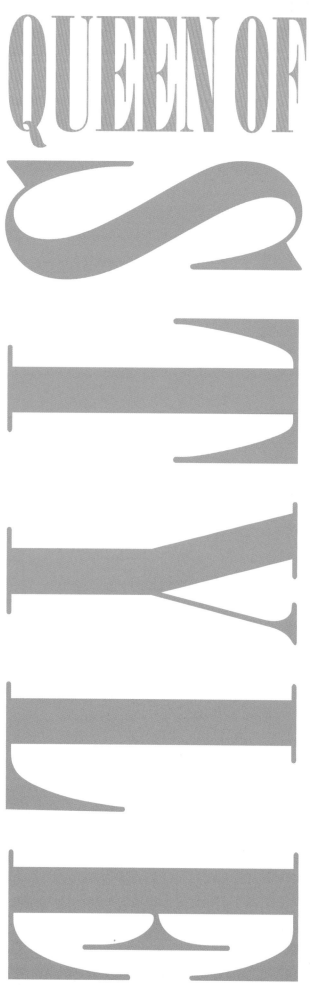

QUEEN OF STYLE

'We have a deep connection to what we wear.'

The Duchess of Sussex in a black bespoke Givenchy one shoulder velvet gown at the British Fashion Awards 2018.

As Meghan's pregnancy progressed, her fashion kudos and sense of style became ever more apparent. Nowhere was this more apparent than at the events commemorating the armistice in November 2019. For the Festival of Remembrance at the Royal Albert Hall, she combined designer with chain store by donning an M&S Collection double crepe bodycon dress with Stella McCartney tie detail coat, black shaggy deer faux leather crossbody bag and her trusty black Manolos. The next morning, Meghan joined other members of the Royal family at the annual Remembrance Sunday commemorations at the Cenotaph in Whitehall, London, wearing a custom black Givenchy coat with caplet detail and with her hair styled in an *'up-do'* with the bun offset to the side. That evening at the Service of Thanksgiving at Westminster Abbey, Meghan was seen in a navy Prada skirt suit, Stephen Jones beret in the same shade and Aquazzura *'Deneuve'* heel in custom navy suede – shoes she also has in black, powder pink and taupe suede.

In two beautiful family photographs released by Clarence House ahead of Prince Charles' 70th birthday on November 14, Meghan wore an off-white sheath dress by Givenchy featuring a

Meghan, Duchess of Sussex attends the annual Remembrance
Sunday Service at The Cenotaph on November 11, 2018 in
London, England

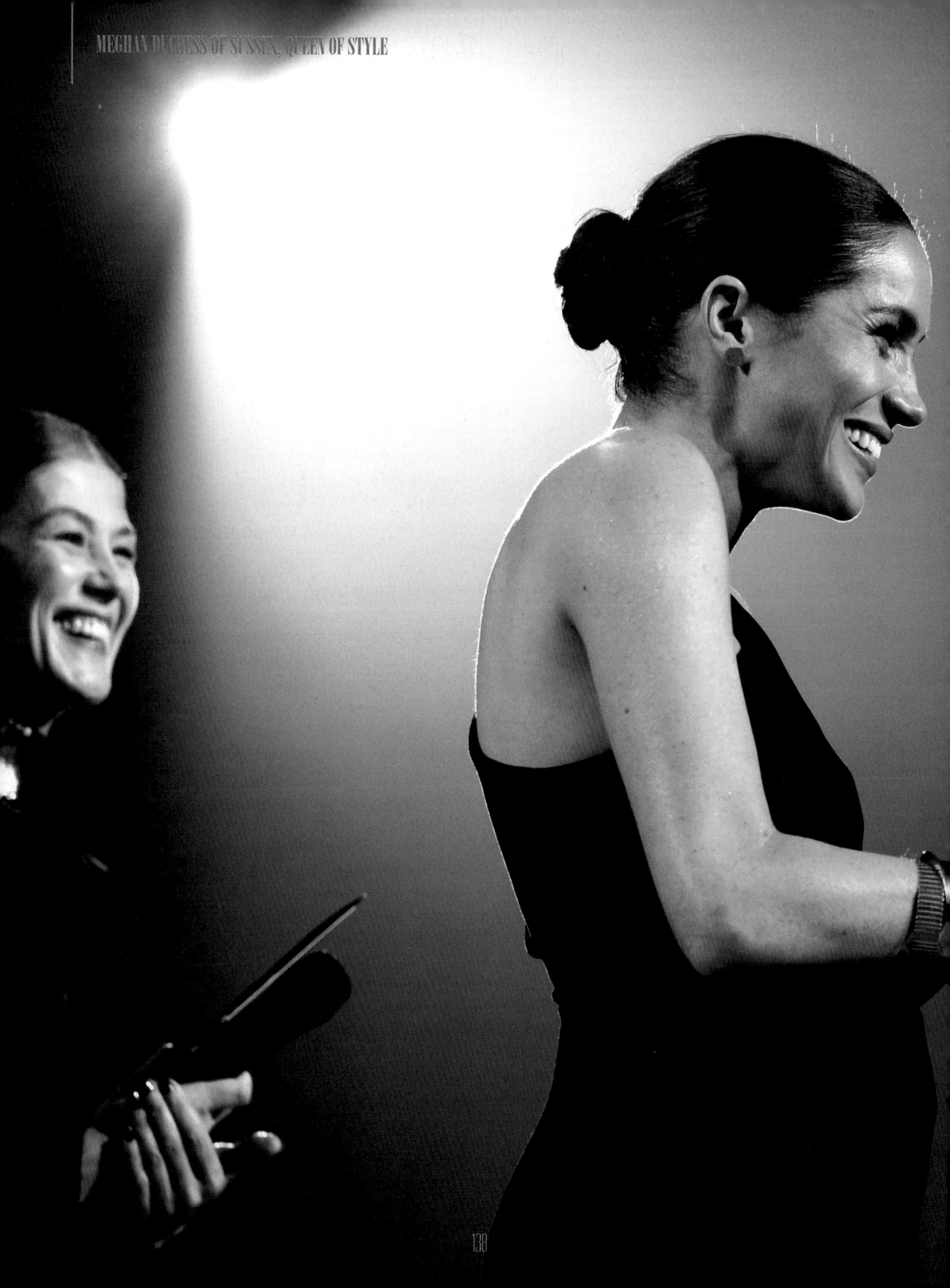

navy neckline, complete with her black Givenchy Double G thin leather belt. She also sported Birks sapphire and double diamond halo drop earrings. Four days later, as Meghan attended her first Royal Variety Performance, the swell of her neat baby bump could be seen beneath the glamorous Safiyaa separates she was wearing – the sparkling, strapless black and white *'Malaya'* and the *'Gayeta'* black maxi skirt. Meghan completed her look with Birks snowflake diamond earrings and Aquazzura heels in black.

Towards the end of November, the Duchess – wearing a Club Monaco *'Daylina'* coat in burgundy, the label's *'Sallyet'* dress and Givenchy black ankle boots – paid a surprise visit to the Hubb Community Kitchen. Meghan was reunited with the women she worked with on the community cookbook, *'Together'*, which sold over 40,000 copies in seven weeks in the UK alone and raised £210,000 for the Hubb kitchen in support of victims of the Grenfell Tower fire. Another *'surprise'* was Meghan's appearance at the British Fashion Awards, where she was greeted with cheers and rapturous applause by the assembled fashionista glitterati. Wearing a stunning Givenchy bespoke one-shoulder gown in black velvet, gold Tamara Mellon *'Karat'* strappy sandals and sporting bangles and earrings by Pippa Small, Meghan presented the

Womanswear Designer of the Year to Claire Waight Keller, the artistic director at Givenchy who created her wedding dress and many other bespoke outfits since Meghan had become the Duchess of Sussex. She revealed her thoughts about fashion in the speech she made at the event.

'We have a deep connection to what we wear. Sometimes it's very personal, sometimes it's emotional. But for me, this connection is rooted in really being able to understand that it's about supporting and empowering each other, especially as women. When we choose to wear a certain designer, we're not just a reflection of their creativity and their vision, but we're also an extension of their values, of something in the fabric, so to speak, that is much more meaningful. I recently read an article that said, "The culture of fashion has shifted from one where it was cool to be cruel to now, where it's cool to be kind."'

Meghan was positively blooming when she paid a festive visit to Brinsworth House in Twickenham to see how the Royal Variety Charity's residential nursing home cares for former entertainers and actors. *'I feel very pregnant today,'* she told residents, wearing a Soia and Kyo *'Adelaida'* ash grey coat, *'Odilia'* floral-print midi dress

Meghan, Duchess of Sussex and Rosamund Pike on stage to present the British Designer of the Year Womenswear Award during The Fashion Awards 2018 in partnership with Swarovski at the Royal Albert Hall on December 10, 2018 in London

by Brock Collection, her Wilbur and Gussie bespoke oyster silk clutch bag, her Aquazzure *'Deneuve'* heels in taupe and Birks *'Petale'* gold and diamond earrings.

At Sandringham for Christmas with the rest of the Royals, Meghan wowed in Victoria Beckham – a deep navy tailored slim coat, navy fit-and-flare V-neck dress, black leather knee-high boots and the VB black powder box bag, complete with Awon Golding millinery *'Vika'* cocktail hat. At five months pregnant, Meghan now felt suited to the former Spice Girl's designs about which, during her *'Suits'* days she had remarked, *'I love Victoria Beckham dresses, but I don't have the long torso to support that silhouette.'*

For her first public engagement of 2019, Meghan made a surprise visit to *'Smart Works'* in West London. She was now Royal Patron of the charity that helps long-term unemployed and vulnerable women regain the confidence they need to get jobs, succeed at job interviews, return to employment and transform their lives. The Duchess harked back to pre-Royal days by wearing Gianvito Rossi *'Plexi'* cow print heels, which had first been seen in a 2015 photo shoot. Carrying a Victoria Beckham mini vanity box bag, she also wore an Oscar de le Renta sand cotton-twill coat over an *'Eliza'*

black knit dress by US maternity label, Hatch. Ariane Goldman, founder of the label, was understandably delighted that the Duchess was wearing one of her designs.

'We actually had no idea she was going to wear our Eliza for her first official maternity look, so it was an awesome surprise,' she said. *'We didn't* send it to her; we think she got it on her own, which is even more flattering. Meghan always looks perfectly polished, and her maternity style is no different. She's made every outfit appear effortless and chic while staying true to herself, and I love that she's showing off her bump as it grows.'

The Duchess was spot on-trend, wearing the contrastingly vibrant colours of purple and scarlet, for her first joint engagement of the year with Prince Harry to Birkenhead, near Liverpool. Meghan sported a Sentaler wide-collar wrap coat in red – a style she also owns in camel – a Babaton *'Maxwell'* dress, a Gabriela Hearst *'Nina'* leather tote handbag and Stuart Weitzman *'Leigh'* red suede heels. The ensemble received a resounding *'thumbs-up'* from fashion editors, including 'Hello' magazine's Hilary Alexander who wrote: *'I love the red Sentaler coat and purple Babaton dress she wore to an official visit in Birkenhead. It was such a striking combination and*

Meghan, Duchess of Sussex visits the National Theatre in central London on January 30, 2019 after it was announced that she would be patron of the theatre

the colour pairing reminded me of an outfit worn by Princess Diana. I wonder if Meghan is echoing some of her style choices'. It was during this engagement that Meghan revealed her baby was due in *'late April or early May'*.

The Duchess rocked a smoky eyed, red-lipped look when she appeared in a show-stopping navy sequinned gown by Roland Mouret to attend the London premiere of Cirque du Soleil's *'Totem'* at the Royal Albert Hall. This she teamed with her Givenchy black satin clutch, Stuart Weitzman black *'Nudist'* sandals and a deeply personal gold cuff bracelet with blue stones that had once belonged to Princess Diana. In contrast, she stepped out in a neutral coordinating set from the spring/summer 2019 collection of American designer Brandon Maxwell to pay her first visit to the National Theatre in London, of which she was now patron having taken over the position from the Queen. Meghan nailed the custom-made V-necked dress, based on a ready-to-wear piece, and shawl collar blazer which she teamed with the Aquazzura *'Matilde'* crisscross nude suede shoes – the very same shoes she had worn to her and Prince Harry's first official photocall together when they announced their engagement in November 2017. 'Elle' magazine were glowing in their praise. *'Meghan is well aware of how flattering teaming a matching colour palette throughout her entire outfit is,'* was their consensus. *'Her tonal dressing styling hack is so easy to emulate and will add some serious sophistication whatever the occasion. Whether she's donning high-end, high street or a passed-on heirloom, Meghan's sartorial prowess knows no bounds.'*

A few days later, Meghan received a rock star welcome as she arrived at City University in London to officially launch the last of her four new patronages – Royal Patron of The Association of Commonwealth Universities. She was greeted by hundreds of screaming students as she stepped out of her official car wearing the black Givenchy coat she had worn on Remembrance Day, a black pleated dress with a high-low hemline, and her Manolo blush heels. For the first time, she wore her hair in a sleek, ballerina type bun. She looked equally incredible in early February when she arrived in Bristol for engagements with Prince Harry, wearing a playful animal-print dress by Oscar de la Renta, Sarah Flint *'Marina'* high-heeled boots in olive green and a dark coat by William Vintage.

Meghan, Duchess of Sussex attends an engagement with the Association of Commonwealth Universities (ACU) at City, University of London on January 31, 2019 in London, England

ABOVE:

Meghan, Duchess of Sussex departs after attending an engagement with the Association of Commonwealth Universities (ACU) at City, University Of London on January 31, 2019 in London, England

RIGHT:

Prince Harry, Duke of Sussex and Meghan, Duchess of Sussex visit a new statue to mark the 100th anniversary of the death of poet Wilfred Owen, which was erected on Hamilton Square in November, during an official visit to Birkenhead on January 14, 2019 in Birkenhead, United Kingdom

ABOVE L:

Meghan, Duchess of Sussex during a visit to The National Theatre on January 30, 2019 in London, England. The Duchess was announced as patron of the National Theatre, one of two patronages passed on by Her Majesty The Queen

ABOVE R:

Meghan, Duchess of Sussex attends a gala performance of 'The Wider Earth' in support of the Queen's Commonwealth Trust & the Queen's Commonwealth Canopy at the Natural History Museum on February 12, 2019 in London, England

OPP. PAGE:

Meghan, Duchess of Sussex visits the Hubb Community Kitchen to see how funds raised by the 'Together: Our Community' cookbook are making a difference at Al Manaar, North Kensington on November 21, 2018 in London, England

MEGHAN'S RARE

FASHION FAILS

Even a style icon like the Duchess makes the occasional mistake...

Labelgate

When the Duchess of Sussex arrived at Fua'amotu airport in Tonga last October, she appeared to have left the label on her red Self-Portrait midi dress. But this wasn't the only occasion Meghan neglected to remove something-that shouldn't have been there from an outfit. Earlier in 2018, she stepped out in Birmingham, UK, in a navy J Crew coat but had failed to remove the X-shaped stitching before slipping it on.

Living Room Curtains?

Meghan wore a floral dress by Oscar de la Renta to a wedding in summer 2018. But the demure, ankle-length number with a wrap front, billowing sleeves and ruffled hem appeared to be too big for her. One comment on Twitter read, *'When wearing Oscar de la Renta makes you look like you are wearing the living room curtains.'* Another advised the Duchess to *'sack the stylist'*.

More Fancy Dress than Period Chic

Meghan wore a striped dress by Australian designer Martin Grant for an official meeting with the Prime Minister of Tonga in October 2018. But fashionistas were not impressed. *'It comes off as being slightly fancy dress and doesn't feel like a 2018 play on Victorian chic, but a more like a recreation of a period piece,'* celebrity stylist and designer Lucas Armitage explains. *'The green and cream colour combo isn't very chic and the whole vibe isn't what I'd expect from Meghan.'*

No to Welly Boots and Blazer

The Duchess donned a blazer by New Zealand designer, Karen Walker, which she paired with J. Crew Toothpick jeans and wellington boots by

Muck as she arrived to dedicate a 20-hectare area of native bush to The Queen's Commonwealth Canopy in Auckland. While there's certainly nothing wrong with wellies, it's the combination with an otherwise polished ensemble that jars. *'I'm all for practical dressing, but whoever thought waterproof boots and a business-like blazer would be a perfect pairing?'* Lucas Armitage asks. *'This was a disjointed look. I would have loved to see her go full-on casual chic in a stylish parka and fine knit.'*

Sheer Nightmare

Meghan turned quite a few heads in one of her last appearances of the tour in New Zealand when she wore a royal blue sweater and skirt combo. Unbeknown to the Duchess, the skirt was completely sheer in the daylight and bared all from the waist down.

What a Heel!

It was with trepidation that the Duchess stepped warily onto the grass at the Windsor Royal Polo Club to support Prince Harry while he played a charity match – and no wonder. Her beige, extremely high-heeled sling-backs by Aquazurra kept piercing the ground as she walked. Flats would have been better.

Demure but Dull

Fashion scribes wondered if Meghan had subdued her usual sassy style when she appeared in this demure – some would say dull – outfit by Goat at her father-in-law's birthday Garden Party. The consensus was that the mesh sleeves looked odd while the dress itself was ill-fitting. Plus, she was wearing the dreaded pantyhose.

Oh Mother!

While it's great to see Meghan combining chain store items with designer pieces, the H&M beige-coloured *'Mama Fine'* knitted dress she stepped out in to visit a dog charity in London when six months pregnant didn't do her many favours. The fabric creased too easily and looked a size too small.

Meghan's striped dress by Australian designer Martin Grant

The former **Meghan Markle** is a Royal who clearly understands and values fashion. She has built relationships with international designer labels with royal connections, from **Givenchy**, her wedding dress designer who was once loved by **Wallis Simpson**, to **Dior** – a one-time favourite of Princess Margaret. Yet she remains faithful to her favourite chain-store brands. Meghan's style is the gift that keeps on giving. It is constantly evolving and is a fascinating fashion choreography. The Duchess is now one of the world's most influential fashion personalities, with the power to spark sell-outs and set trends – more so than any other Royal female, past or present.

That's Meghan – Duchess of Sussex, Queen of Style.